OPENING TIME

A PUBGOER'S COMPANION

OPENING TIME

A PUBGOER'S COMPANION

IF YOU WANT
**A Prime Glass of Ale
For a Penny,**
Go to *The Crown and Still,*
(**The Old Red House
New Revived!**)
15, Clare Street,
Clare Market,
WHERE YOU MAY ALSO GET A
Sandwich for **NOTHING** ! ! !
Unadulterated Porter 3d per pot
And the *Best Gin* in the Market.

Anthony Burton

UNWIN HYMAN
London   Sydney

First published in Great Britain by
Unwin Hyman, an imprint of Unwin Hyman Limited, 1987

UNWIN HYMAN LIMITED
Denmark House
37–39 Queen Elizabeth Street
London SE1 2QB

and

40 Museum Street
London WC1A 1LU

Allen & Unwin Australia Pty Ltd
8 Napier Street
North Sydney
NSW 2060
Australia

Allen & Unwin with the Port Nicholson Press
60 Cambridge Terrace
Wellington
New Zealand

British Library Cataloguing in Publication Data
Burton, Anthony
    Opening time: a pubgoer's companion.
    1. Hotels, taverns, etc.——England
    I. Title
    647'.9542   TX950.59.G7

ISBN 0 04 440044 6

Typeset in Great Britain by
Cambridge Photosetting Services
Printed and bound in Great Britain by
St Edmundsbury Press Limited,
Bury St Edmunds, Suffolk

CONTENTS

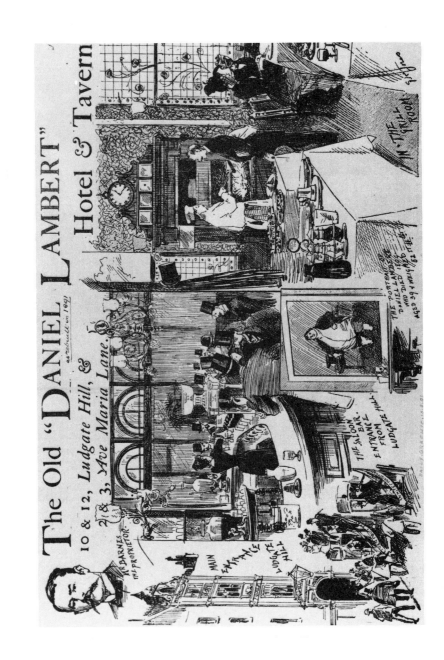

The Old "DANIEL LAMBERT" as built in 1891.

Hotel & Tavern

10 & 12, Ludgate Hill, &
2, & 3, Ave Maria Lane.

W. BARNES.
THE PROPRIETOR.

MAIN ENTRANCE

LUDGATE HILL

THE SALOON BAR.
ENTRANCE FROM HILL
LUDGATE HILL.

THE PORTRAIT OF
DANIEL LAMBERT 1806
WHO DIED 1809
AGED 39 4 WEIGHED 52 ST.

IN THE
GRILL ROOM

1. Beer and Britannia

The inns of England are the best in Europe, those of
Canterbury are the best in England, and the Fountain,
wherein I am now lodged as handsomely as I was in the
King's Palace, the best in Canterbury.

I certainly would not argue with the general view, though inns
have changed a little since those lines were penned in 1129, not by
a xenophobic Englishman but by an ambassador from Germany.
But what is it that makes the British pub "the best", what gives it
its unique character? Why, indeed, go to a pub at all? An obvious
answer would be "to get a drink", and not just any old drink. As,
coming somewhat closer to our own time, the Rev. Sydney Smith
put it: "What two ideas are more inseparable than Beer and
Britannia?" True enough, but you don't actually have to go to a
pub in order to drink beer or whatever else takes your fancy. You
can stock up the drinks cupboard at home and enjoy your tipple
at leisure and probably at less cost. Then, should you run out in
the course of your imbibing, the stock can be replenished at the
grocer's, the supermarket, or the off licence, and you won't even
have to wait for the hours decreed by our curious and archaic
licensing laws. No, if drinking was all there was to it, you would
be better off staying in the comfort of home. Yet we do still go to
the pub: why?
   One of the principal attractions of the pub for me is that it still
offers company in a way that almost no other British institution
does. Where else can you appear as a complete stranger and at
once be able to join in a conversation and, just as importantly,
where else can you meet such a diverse group of people? Until
recently, I lived in a village near Oxford and I would regularly
wander down to the local for a pint and a chat with the other
habitués. They were a pretty mixed group. For a start, as all
respectable village pubs with any pretensions to being considered
genuine locals must, it possessed an authorized Old Character.

We had George, who occupied a seat by the door – and it was not a good idea to try and sit there before he arrived, for he was quite liable to give you a decidedly sharp proprietorial reminder with his walking stick. His conversation would have delighted any serious student of dialect English, though to my ears it often sounded like a bad rehearsal for *The Archers*. He was always especially keen to provide a personal comment on any aspect of local history, though he was not, truth to tell, the most reliable of witnesses. We were once discussing an accident which occurred when a passenger train crashed over a bridge and fell into the frozen Oxford Canal. George declared that he remembered it well and provided convincing details. This was a little surprising as the accident occurred in 1874, and even George was not that old. A somewhat cantankerous old gentleman perhaps, but the pub cared for him: if he failed to appear for his regular lunchtime session, then someone was despatched up to the cottage to check that he was all right. George provided the pub with its Character, the pub provided George with care and attention. When he died a successor appeared as if he had only been waiting in the wings for his turn to stride into centre stage. Johnny's specialities were old photographs and reminiscences, with which he would delight visitors and exasperate locals. You could almost hear a groan go round the bar as the pictures were produced and the all too familiar descriptions began.

It is a poor sort of village pub that doesn't have its George or Johnny, but they are only a part of the cast list. Other characters might prove more surprising. I would frequently chat and drink with two other regulars and I cannot think of anywhere but the village pub where all three of us could meet – a writer, a distinguished professor of philosophy and an Irish gardener. Our conversations together were at least as good a reason for visiting the pub as the promise of a pint of bitter.

It is easy to over-glamorize this aspect of pub life and I am not going to pretend that anyone walking into a public bar will necessarily find a gardener, a philosopher and an author discussing English literature – indeed our own trio was more likely to be debating the growth of beetroot than the theories of Bentham.

There is a popular view of the general banality of pub conversation which was expressed with both wit and accuracy by T. S. Eliot in *The Waste Land* – a passage that, if it does nothing else, proves that modern poets are, indeed, a part of common humanity.

When Lil's husband got demobbed, I said –
I didn't mince my words, I said to her myself,
HURRY UP PLEASE IT'S TIME
Now Albert's coming back, make yourself a bit smart.
He'll want to know what you done with that money he gave you
To get yourself some teeth. He did, I was there.
You have them all out, Lil, and get a nice set,
He said, I swear, I can't bear to look at you.
And no more can't I, and think of poor Albert,
He's been in the army four years, he wants a good time,
And if you don't give it him, there's others will, I said.
Oh is there, she said. Something o' that, I said.
Then I'll know who to thank, she said, and give me a straight look.
HURRY UP PLEASE IT'S TIME

Now, that might seem a touch over the top, but listen to a real conversation in a real pub, and you will very soon have to acknowledge that it is not far off the mark. The trouble is that few of us have the inclination or the patience to record such chats. But, in the great days of documentary recording in the thirties and forties the experts set out, notebooks in hand to preserve pub chat for posterity. The result can be found in a remarkable book, *The Pub and the People* produced by Mass Observation in 1943, the product of three years work in what is somewhat coyly described as "Worktown". Very little detective work is needed to identify this Lancashire cotton town, described as having 300 pubs, 200 churches, 24 prostitutes and 180,000 other citizens as Bolton. What is not recorded are the heroic efforts put in by the researchers. Sir John Betjeman had his own views on that, expressed in *The Dear Old Village*:

Go to the Inn on any Friday night
And listen to them while they're getting tight
At the expense of him who stands them drinks,
The Mass-Observer with the Hillman Minx.
(Unwitting he of all the knowing winks)
The more he circulates the bitter ales
The longer and the taller grow the tales.
"Ah! this is England," thinks he, "rich and pure
As tilth and loam and wains and horse-manure,
Slow – yes. But sociologically sound."
"Landlord!" he cries
"The same again all round!"

They were not as naïve as Betjeman made out. One cannot help wondering how many pints the intrepid recorder had to drink – and stand – before he came up with this superb gem of pub conversation, as fresh today as it was nearly half a century ago. The topic that began it all was the local swimming baths, but it soon broadened out to a general discussion of swimming – except for The Oldest Inhabitant who doggedly stuck to the first topic:

X: "I'll tell you 'oo were a good lad: Bob Robbins . . . that lad could fly through t'water like a bloody fish."
Y: "Bill Howard, that's 'is name."
X: "Goes into water like a bloody fish."
Old man (loud): "I remember it being built."
X: "I'll tell you what 'e could do – you know when you're walking along the towing path, you an' me walking along the towing path, e'd keep up wi' you, you an' me, walking decent tha knows, e'll keep up wi' you"
X stops, drinks, and the old man can be heard stubbornly reiterating: "I remember it being built."
X: "I'll tell you the hardest feat that was ever known – for a man to fall off the top of the bath and not go to the bottom

and not go to the top, as long as 'e can 'old 'is breath – I've
seen (name inaudible) do that. 'e could do a 'undred yards
in eleven seconds – wi'out any training. What could 'e do
wi' training? I'm telling you, he could stay in t'water, not
to go to the top and not go to the bottom – an' I'll tell you
'ow 'e did it."

Y (interrupting): "'ave another."

X: "Aye."

While he is getting his drink the chap stands up, and says "I
swim that road", demonstrating convulsive side stroke
movements with his arms.

The old man looks up from his argument and remarks "I go
left 'and first". And returns to the swimming bath
discussion.

Any pub regular will instantly recognize the conversation. The
topic may change, but the wonderful mixture of improbability
and inconsequentiality can still be heard throughout the land. The
great thing about such conversations is that anyone can join in.
They are free-for-alls, open to the entire community of the pub.

It is not perhaps always quite that easy for a stranger to wriggle
away into general conversation, and this is where the landlord or
landlady puts in an appearance as the catalyst who makes the
reaction possible. Pubs may change, drinks may change, customers may change – but the innkeepers remain as the still point in
this turning world. It is on them that the responsibility falls of
making a stranger welcome: they have the job of pulling the
company together into a harmonious, cheerful whole. It is the
modern landlord's job just as it was the job of the landlord of The
Tabard in *The Canterbury Tales*. Chaucer's Host is instantly
recognizable, for you can find him still in a hundred pubs – a man
of "girth a little wide" chatty but tactful, joking with the
customers, talking about sport, flattering his guests by just the
right amount to get them talking. Anyone opening the door of an
unknown pub in a strange town who finds such a character
behind the bar should give thanks for his good fortune. It is not
always the owner or landlord who is found hauling on the beer

pump handle: there was a time when the bar maid was the great lure – though conversational ability was not always the greatest attraction. The indefatigable researchers of Mass Observation were assiduous in their studies of this intriguing phenomenon. Here is our man at the end of a tiring evening's work:

> Observer leaves in company with two youthful drunks, who have been playing darts and flirting with the barmaid from 8.30 until just before closing time. She accompanies the group to the lobby and then on to the doorstep. One of the drunks and the observer both kiss her goodnight. The kisses were long and interesting.

Such are the hardships the researcher must undergo in the course of duty.

Why should it be that general chat is so much easier in a pub than elsewhere? Part of the answer must lie in the lubricating effect of alcohol on the tongue, but it is also due in no small measure to the particular design of the building itself. In the pub, you approach the bar to order your drinks; after that you can stay propping up the counter, wander round or sit in a quiet corner just as you choose. In cafe or restaurant, the staff come to you, take your order and expect to find you in the same place when they come back again with the food. The pub gives flexibility, but the main secret of sociability lies with the bar and the inevitable group that surrounds it. There is a well established custom which provides at least the opening opportunity for conversation. The new arrival has a number of conversational gambits. There is that ever faithful topic, the weather, which on a day in, say, July can either be:

> "I suppose we have to call this summer!"

Or:

> "It looks like we finally got some decent weather."

12

Should there happen to be a test match in progress, this can be followed up by: "I expect England are happy enough" in the first case or "They must be praying for rain" in the second, since it is better than even odds that the national team are looking for bad weather to save the match. Contrary to general opinion, cricket is still an accepted topic of conversation, for though attendance at matches may have dropped, comment in the public bar has remained at a high level. Once firmly set in on weather and sport, you are on your own and well set for a good conversational canter.

The corollary to this openness of conversation is that you are liable to find yourself prey to the pub bore. Just as the village ancient is a stalwart member of the pub company, so too is the perennial pest. Everyone has their own particular aversion. Top of my list is the car bore, obsessed with the minutiae of the internal combustion engine. I only have to hear a phrase such as, "of course, mine's the 1.6 with the overhead cam" to go into instant switch-off. On the other hand, a snatch of conversation containing the words "slide valve on the low pressure cylinder" will find me an eager participant in talking shop with another steam buff. Which proves the old saying that one man's fellow enthusiast is another man's crashing bore. One could go on listing manifestations of the pub bore forever, from the one who retells the jokes heard last night on the telly, undeterred by a chorus announcing that absolutely everyone present had already seen the show and heard the jokes, to the other one who starts off: "You know what's wrong with this country don't you?" What you do indeed know is that he will supply the answer himself in a harangue where ignorance and bigotry are nicely balanced. But this is a celebration, not a wake so let us not dwell too long on the bores, though it is worth noting that the pub is a tolerant place, probably because one knows that for every bore there is also likely to be a fascinating character. Chance encounters can often lead to that most satisfying of entertainments – good conversation.

Chat and drinks are the two main items provided by the pub, though these days food is becoming increasingly important, rather too much so in some cases. I recently visited a pub in Dorset which had a vast blackboard with a chalked up menu: unfortunately there was only one person behind the bar who, whenever food was ordered, disappeared to cook it. A passing motorist called in with small boy in tow to inquire if the child could be allowed on to the premises. "Don't worry", a laconic regular assured the visitor, "by the time you get served in here, he'll be old enough to order a pint". Games too have their place, and have done for centuries. Indeed, the pub sign "The Chequers" is generally thought to date back to Roman times where it indicated a tavern where games could be played. Support for the theory comes from finding a similar sign in Pompeii. But these are, to my mind, subsidiary attractions: I like a snack at lunchtime and I enjoy a game of darts, but first and foremost I look for good company and good beer – and the latter is at least as important as the former.

The drinking of beer in a public house is not compulsory, but as any publican will tell you, beer remains the mainstay of the trade – and it is to beer that I will always turn for preference in a British pub. Other countries have their own delights to offer and sometimes we try to emulate them. We now have wine bars where for a mere pound or so you can buy a glass of plonk that would cost around ten pence in a French cafe. Recently, too, a number of perfectly decent pubs have been converted to establishments selling violently coloured concoctions in glasses which sprout odd shaped straws and tiny parasols. I am a great believer in sticking to the wine of the country. I have the happiest memories of sipping wine in bars in France or, on colder days, indulging in that instant central heating system, the cafe cognac. I look back with equal pleasure on sipping ice cold dry martinis in New York, made as they should be made with the merest slurp of vermouth in a glass of gin. No two people, of course, can ever agree on the ideal martini and some purists contend that passing the corked bottle of vermouth over the glass of gin is quite sufficient. Or again, there are whisky sours consumed in a hot, smoky jazz club in New Orleans – and the list could be extended for as far as travelling takes you. But you cannot export the experience: the

14

robust peasant wine you enjoyed in Provence becomes just another rough red with an after-taste that leaves your teeth feeling as though they have just been sandpapered when you try the same drink at home. The whisky sour that tasted so good at 3 am at Crazy Shirleys when the band were playing for themselves and the coach tours had left, just seems plain sour when the music has stopped.

Beer is the perfect drink for the pub. It comes in large measures so that just one glass provides plenty of conversation time. It is a drink of great variety and subtlety, but above all perhaps it has that special quality of belonging: just as a Chianti drunk in the open air with a view over the hills of Tuscany will taste better than any Chianti drunk anywhere else in the world, so too a pint of, say, Hook Norton consumed in an old Cotswold village pub will give a special pleasure. Not that beer is quite the universal British drink, as cider drinkers in the West Country will be quick to point out. And there is the other truly great British drink – whisky – but much as I enjoy savouring the delights of good malt, it is not, for my taste, a drink for the pub. Several million Scotsmen disagree, but even they very largely take their dram with an accompanying glass of something longer. I can rhapsodize over my favourite malts, comparing the peaty brews of Islay with the rich smoothness of the Spey – and a glass of malt after a good meal counts as one of life's great pleasures. But for an everyday drink in an everyday pub, I go along with an advertising slogan that first appeared back in the 1930s – Beer is Best.

Perhaps we can begin to see an answer to the question posed at the beginning of this little introduction – what makes the British pub special? It is a combination of different factors which we can now look at in more detail. But what of the particular question posed at the beginning? What made the Fountain the best of them all? There, I am afraid, all is silence. The inn so much admired by a German visitor in the twelfth century was demolished by a second German visitor in the twentieth, when he dropped his bombs on Canterbury in the Second World War. There have been other changes, if not quite so sudden and dramatic, that have affected the British pub and British beer.

Tending hops – an illustration from Reynolde Scot's book of 1574.

2. The True and Proper Drink

Good ale is the true and proper drink of the Englishman.
George Borrow, Wild Wales

These are the sentiments expressed forcibly and more recently by that most excellent body The Campaign for Real Ale (CAMRA). Alarmed at the growth of the big brewers through a series of mergers and takeovers, which involved a steady reduction in the number of beers available accompanied by a no less determined move towards keg beers at the expense of cask conditioned beers, they declared enough was enough. Battle was joined, and all over Britain the beer drinkers rallied to the cause in what was to prove and is still proving a remarkably, indeed incredibly, successful war against the giants. The lowly drinkers rose in their wrath against the mighty brewers and gained more successes than even their best friends thought possible. But what was the fuss all about? Why should the downtrodden masses respond not to a call for liberty, equality and fraternity but for gravity, hand pump and diversity? Just how traditional was traditional ale and in what way was it more real than a pint of lager or Watney's Red Barrel? If tradition implies that something has been around for a very long time, then British beer can certainly qualify. But when the old gaffer in the corner sadly shakes his head and intones the time honoured incantation – "Beer's not what it used to be" – agree with him. You could even add – "Beer never was what it used to be", for the story of British beer is one of continuous change.

The brewing of beer is essentially very simple. A cereal grain, such as barley, is an energy storehouse ready to be tapped as soon as the grain begins to grow. This energy is packed into starch which, when the seed germinates, is broken down by an enzyme into malt-sugar. Sugar is the chemical form that the growing seed can use directly. But stop the seed growing and the malt-sugar can be extracted with water, the sugary liquid can then be fermented with yeast to produce beer. Other substances might be added for flavour or to help in preservation but that, in its essentials, is brewing. If that was really all there was to it we could end the chapter right here, but brewing is a little more complex than that. It is indeed a subject of infinite variety. Just as all makers of wine pulp grapes and then ferment the juice, but in the process can produce anything from the richest claret to the Eurogrape mediocrity of the vinegary subordinaire, so too the brewers can produce anything from a dark, full bodied stout to palest, tasteless fizz. We shall look at some of these subtleties later, but when did it all start and where?

We do at least know where and when the oldest records of beer production occurred, for brewing is recorded in Mesopotamia five thousand years ago. I can well understand how, once the process had been proven, the Mesopotamians got into production in a big way, but the thing I always find most intriguing is the question of how it ever started off in the first place. I would not wander down to the fields to pick some strange grain and then decide to let it grow a bit, then boil it up for a while and then chuck in some rather nasty malodorous stuff called yeast and finish up drinking it. It all seems hopelessly unlikely. We shall never know quite how it all happened, though there are a good few theories around. The likeliest version goes like this.

Cereal grains in their natural state are pretty indigestible and not especially appetizing objects, and it must have soon become evident that an accidental soaking brought about a great improvement. It tasted better and the seed was a lot more nutritious after partial germination. Then if the seed was dried it could be kept for quite a long while and used as a sort of instant food for travellers, and it could be mixed up with tasty things like honey and herbs and spices to make a form of bread. Now the next part is the really interesting bit. You can imagine a traveller stuck with a load of this bread which had become hardened and pretty disgusting. A frugal sort of chap, he didn't feel like throwing it to the ducks so he decided to give it another good soaking. Now, having been kept around in some less than wholly hygienic containers some interesting organisms could have collected on the bread and our traveller would find his well soaked crumbs beginning to bubble. He might have left it a while out of curiosity by which time the bread would have become a soggy mass and even less appetizing than it had been before. So, rather than give up the whole thing as a dead loss, he tasted the liquid. And the miracle happened. A pleasant sense of well-being pervaded his system, he became more talkative than usual and the more he drank the more garrulous he sounded and the cheerier he felt. He had made beer.

A few thousand years later, a treatise in Norman French described just the same process. It begins, in translation:

> Ale shall now engage my pen
> To set at rest the hearts of men.
> First, my friend your candle light
> Next of spiced cake take a bite

It ends:

> Then, oh miracles and marvels
> Of one candle it makes two candles.

Or, for the erudite among the readers, who prefer the original:

> Ky fet miracles e marveyles
> De une chaundelie deus chandelis.

Whether that was the way of it or not we shall never know, but we do know that "beer-bread" was made and used in much this way around 3000 BC. Yeast was discovered at much the same time, making fermentation less of a hit and miss affair. Once the discovery had been made, the ancients set about making beer with a good will and the texts record eight different types of beer made from malted barley, eight from varieties of wheat and three from various mixtures – Sumeric forerunners of mild and bitter. The news spread, but the southern Europeans soon began to concentrate on fermenting the juice of the grape and storing the resulting wine in earthenware jars, leaving the north Europeans to make beer and keep it in wooden barrels. Among those enthusiastic northerners were the inhabitants of the British Isles. The Mediterraneans met the northerners when the Roman troops invaded these lands, and the southern winebibbers were not particularly impressed by British ale. The Emperor Julian wrote some unflattering verses on our national beverage:

Who made you and from what,
By the true Bacchus, I know not
For he smells of nectar
And you smell of goat.

It probably reads better in the original.

By now, one might assume, that the true British ale had arrived, a brew which had passed that most stringent of tests, that of being liked at home whilst being despised abroad. This, however, was very far from being anything but a distant relation of that real ale which is so vigorously defended by the modern enthusiast. The essential feature of the original old ale was that it should be an unadulterated beverage of malt, water and yeast – the stronger ales being dark, heavy and, to a modern palate, somewhat sweet and sickly. This, for centuries, was ale. Words can be very confusing here, however, for they change sides and one gets odd linguistic changes: this ale was known in Saxon times as beer, but in Norman times as ale again, while if you brewed a second time to produce a weak liquid that was almost devoid of alcohol this was at first called beer and later small beer. So that when one reads, for example, that Elizabeth I quaffed several quarts for breakfast and that the monks of Canterbury had an allowance of eight pints a day, we should not presume that Her Majesty was paralytic by lunchtime nor that the good clerics were never sober. Small beer was so weak that it could probably be sold to small children under today's licensing laws.

Who brewed the ales of old? The short answer is almost everybody – households brewed for their own use, monasteries brewed for themselves and to provide sustenance for travellers, the great houses brewed for everyone on the estate and a few professional brewers produced ale for sale. Home brewing was once so commonplace that it scarcely received comment: it was as much a part of the normal life of the home as the baking of bread. But in 1759 *The London and County Brewer*'s anonymous authors thought it necessary to encourage the readers:

> Here I am to treat of the main Article of showing the Difference between brewing our own Ales and Beers, and buying them, which I doubt not will appear so plain and evident, as to convince any Reader, that many persons may save well towards half in half, and have their Beer and Ale strong, fine, and aged, at their own Discretion.

And by the early nineteenth century that great champion of traditional cottage life William Cobbett was shaking his head sadly over the changed times.

> To show Englishmen, forty years ago, that it was good for them to brew beer in their houses, would have been as impertinent as gravely to insist that they ought to endeavour not to lose their breath; for in those times, to have a *house* and not to brew was a rare thing indeed . . . now there is not one that does it, except by chance the malt be given him.

You did not, however, always even need malt for home brewing. Ale could take many forms, not all of them by any means sticking to the "correct recipe". A sixteenth-century writer who described himself as a "poore man" described how his wife used to reduce the cost of their beer by adding wheatmeal and oats, "and so temperate or mixeth them with the malt that you cannot easily discerne the one from the other". In this way, she was able to brew two hundred gallons of beer a year for £1 out of an income of £40 – which at today's rates would probably work out at just over ten pence a pint – not bad for something that would at least approximate to genuine ale.

Ancient writers speak of a variety of odd drinks such as "gale beer", not as you might think one of those wind-inducing concoctions all too readily available, but a beer made from gale or bog myrtle, a plant which was widely cultivated for the purpose in Saxon Britain. Dorothy Hartley in her excellent book *Food in England*, which quite properly includes nourishing beverages, found gale beer being advertised for sale in Yorkshire as recently as 1863. The beer is made by boiling up the plant with honey and then fermenting the resulting liquid. She also lists several other old country recipes including mangel wurzle beer which seemed as if it would be uniquely appalling until I came across the recipe for cock ale. All you need for that is a standard brew of ale and one large, preferably ancient cockerel. Kill the cockerel, gut it and pound the beast up with a mortar and then stuff the whole lot making sure all the blood goes in, into a canvas bag which you then dunk in the fermenting ale. That is cock ale – and welcome to it. Such, literally, bloodthirsty practices were not normal, but there seems no end to the variations in beer. An American recipe given in the *London and County Brewer* describes ginger beer made from ginger, molasses, yeast and water – not the stuff for children's parties, for the accent falls as much on the beer as on the ginger. A problem which affected all home brewers was that of how to keep the beer in good condition. The simple answer would seem to be – look after your cellar, but some exotic remedies were available for coping with bad ale. You could mix holy water in the brew, add ground ivy (also known as ale cost) ivory shavings or oyster shells. My favourite unlikely recipe is to put lupins under the ale vat. Sadly, the author gives no hint of how this is supposed to work.

These somethat bizarre recipes were presumably looked on askance in the great stately homes and mansions, where the brewing of beer almost took on the nature of an industry. Beer was supplied for the grandees above stairs and for the servants below and was considered an absolutely essential part of the diet for the workers in the fields at harvest time. Something of the atmosphere of those days lingers in the servants' hall at Chirk Castle in Clwyd. The castle itself was originally built as a border fortress in the thirteenth century, but as times settled down, the emphasis moved from defence to comfort and this room which started off as a dining hall in 1529 was later relegated to its more humble function. Beer played an important part in the life of the servants' hall, and the beer trolley is still on show, a tiny barrel on wheels that could be trundled up and down the plain boards of the table at meal times. An inscription on the wall lays down the rules of behaviour:

No Noise, No Strife, Nor Swear at All
But All be Decent in the Hall.

Failure to abide by the rules brought instant retribution: the beer ration was stopped. So order prevailed in the strict hierarchy of the servants' hall, where everything was governed by rank – how close you could sit to the fire and of course how large a share you got of the beer ration. The ale itself was readily available for the hall was right next door to the brewhouse. Some idea of the importance of the place can be gauged by the fact that in that other important mark of hierarchical distinctions - pay - only the head gardener stood above the head brewer and the under brewer. They produced, the records tell us, good malt liquor and a special brew of small beer for the field workers at harvest time.

One of the oldest surviving country house breweries must be that at Lacock Abbey in Wiltshire, which was built when Sir William Sherington acquired the property in 1539. Sadly, it no longer brews but it is quite complete, and there is no reason whatsoever that one can see why it could not be started up again tomorrow. It is very much of its time, with stone flagged floors and little diamond paned windows let into the thick stone walls. The brewing equipment is plain and simple, and remarkably labour saving. The boiler is on a platform and the liquor flows down to a cooler, on down again to the fermenting vessel and the final stage is reached when the beer bucket is placed in a special hole in the ground beneath the big wooden fermenting vat. I am not sure, however, what a modern health inspector would make of the lead linings.

Perhaps the most important institution in the early world of brewing was the church. As a lad, I lived near Fountains Abbey in Yorkshire which, in its day, was the richest Cistercian house in Britain, and there among the ruins you could see the traces of malt house and brewery which were turning out an average of six barrels of good strong ale a day. It does not seem to fit easily with the notion of a monastery in a remote Yorkshire dale founded by thirteen monks from York because they found life in the city was getting too soft. But at the height of its powers, this was a great force in the land farming great stretches of Yorkshire with the help of some five hundred lay brothers. Allowing for the occasional visitor, a little mental arithmetic suggests that they would be quaffing thirty pints a day per person which seems a little unlikely. The abbey must have been a major brewer for the whole area. But that was only one aspect of the church's involvement with ale.

Church festivals required the brewing of special ales, and the ales became such an important part of the proceedings that they eventually gave their name to the festivals themselves, which became Church Ales. So we find Gower in the prologue to Shakespeare's *Pericles*, prefacing his story with these words:

It hath been sung at festivals
On ember days, and holy ales.

The greatest of these festivals was Whitsuntide, the holiday based on White Sunday, the day which has sadly passed from the calendar of British festivals to be replaced by boring Spring Bank Holiday Monday. The Whitsun Ale was, in its day, a great event; a time of celebration which gave the church an opportunity to replenish its coffers. Cakes were made for sale just as they are in every village fête and bring-and-buy sale, but the real money spinner was the ale brewed for the occasion, the Whitsun Ale itself. Local rules laid down just how much the villagers were expected to brew, stipulated just what quality was expected and called for wardens to be appointed to oversee the whole affair. Every adult in the community was expected to attend, and the

24

church officials turned a politic eye away from some of the excesses, for it was all helping to swell the funds.

Some clergy were more helpful than others in this charitable work and on a scandalous occasion at Limington in Somerset the vicar was so particularly helpful that he finished up in the village stocks, an undignified start for the career of a man who was later to become one of the most famous and powerful in England, Cardinal Wolsey. The Church Ales developed a reputation for being roisterous, drunken affairs which inevitably attracted criticism as puritanical views became more popular. Shakespeare has Sir Toby Belch speak up for the old tradition against the new strictures when he attacks Malvolio:

> Dost thou think, because thou art virtuous, there shall be no more cakes and ale?

But the cakes and ale of the Whitsun feast were disappearing. They lingered on in a Whitsun ceremony at Woodstock, near Oxford, where a Whitsun Ale was held every seven years in a somewhat decorous form up to 1843. A maypole was put up, a lord and lady were elected and they toured the town accompanied by a painted wooden horse and morris dancers, and a huge cake was baked and pieces sold off. The one thing that was missing was the ale. It all seems to have very little to do with the boisterous holiday mood of the genuine old Church Ales. Somehow, one cannot quite see the Church of England reviving a festival in which they presided over a grand, official booze up.

It was not just "cakes and ale" that were under threat by the sixteenth century, the old English ale itself was being attacked by a foreign import – beer. This is distinguished from ale by the use of hops, which help to preserve the drink and give it a distinctive bitter flavour. A popular rhyme, of which there are numerous variations, has it that:

> Hops, reformation, bay and beer
> Came into England all in one year.

25

That would be 1520 but well-known as the rhyme may be it is far from accurate. European beer, made with hops, was certainly reaching Britain as early as Richard III's reign, for a petition presented by the Brewers' Company complained of the "sotill and crafty means of foreyns . . . puttying of hoppes and other things in the said ale, contrary to the good and holesome manner of bruynge of ale of old tyme used." The same document, incidentally, is first to use the word "liquor" for the water used in brewing, a term now universally applied in the industry. This was the first shot in the medieval Campaign for Real Ale. But the real battles were to take place in the sixteenth century when hopped beer suddenly seemed to increase its popularity, probably helped by the arrival of Flemish immigrants. Protagonists stated their cases with great vigour and considerable nationalistic fervour. Andrew Boorde in his book of 1542, *A Compendyous Regyment or a Dyetary of Helth* praised the virtues of traditional ale:

> Ale is made of malte and water, and they the which do put any other thynge to ale than is rehersed, except yest, barme, o godesgood doth sofystical theyr ale. Ale for an englysshe-man is a naturall drink. Ale must have these propertyes, it must be fresshe and cleare, it must not be ropy or smoky . . . Barley malte maketh better ale than oten malte or any other coine doth, it doth ingendre grose humoures, but yette it maketh a man stronge.

He then proceeded to attack the filthy foreign muck that was threatening to take its place:

> Bere is made of malte, of hoppes, and water, it is a natural drynke for a dutche man. And now of late dayes it is moche used in England to the detryment of many englys: the men, specyally it kylleth them, the which be troubled with the colyeke and the stone and the strangulation, for the drynke is a cold drynke: yet it doth make a man fat, and doth inflate the bely, as it doth appere by the dutche mens faces & belyes.

Another stalwart supporter of real ale was John Taylor, a gentleman whose acquaintance I first met in a quite different context as "the waterman poet". He was in fact a working Thames waterman in the early seventeenth century in the days when the river was still the great highway of London. He was one of those who rowed passengers from place to place, a kind of waterborne London cabby. It was an occupation very liable to give rise to some powerful thirsts, best satisfied by ale. He had no time for those who took a dislike to the ancient brew:

> This humour moved the scurrilous pen of a shamelesse writer in the reign of King Henry the third, detractingly to inveigh against this unequal'd liquor.
> Thus
> For muddy, foggy, fulsome, puddle, stinking
> For all of these, Ale is the onely drinking.
> Of all the authors that I have ever yet read, this is the onely one that hath attempted to brand the glorious splendour of that Ale beloved decoction; but observe this fellow, by the perpetuall use of water (which was his accustomed drinke) he fell into such convulsion and lethargick diseases, that he remained in opinion a dead man; however the knowing Physicians of that time, by the frequent and inward application of *Ale*, not only recovered him to his pristine estate of health, but also enobled him in body and braine for the future, that he became famous in his writings, which for the most part were afterwards spent with much *Aleoquent* and *Aleborate* commendation.

A fine moral tale this, which was set out in a little piece called *Drinke and Welcome* which appeared in 1637 and which lists the virtues of ale, ending:

> It is as much a nourisher of Mankinde, that if my mouth were as bigge as Bishopgate, my Pen as long as a Maypole, and my Inke a flowing spring, or a standing fishpond, yet I could not with Mouth, Pen, or Inke, speake or write the true worth and worthiness of *Ale*.

But if he was an enthusiast for traditional ale, he was no lover of the foreign additives. "Hop comes crawling lamely in", he said, "and makes a Bitter difference". Other were even more scathing and popular rhymes made dire predictions:

> For to speak of killing, that I am not willing,
> For that in a manner were but to rail,
> But Beer hath its name 'cos it brings to the Bier,
> Therefore, well fare, say I, to a pot of good ale.

There were voices raised on the other side as well, if seldom as forcefully; but then, the defenders of beer had no need to be excessively strident, their side was clearly winning the battle. Reynolde Scot author of *A Perfite platforme of a Hoppe Garden* (1574) sought to combine the best of the old, by encouraging home brewing, with the best of the new, by setting aside land for growing hops:

> Me thinkes I might aptlye compare such men as have grounde fitte for this purpose, and will not employ it accordingly, to Alehouse Knightes, partly for the small devotion which doth the one and the other have unto Hoppes, but especially for that many of these Ale Knights having good drinke at home of their owne, can be content to drinke worse abroade at an Alehouse.

He won half the argument: hopped beer completely displaced the old ale, but home brew gave way before the inroads of the professionals. Hardly had that battle been won, however, before a new enemy appeared over the horizon: the Demon Gin.

> All fiery spirits damn'd, I need not tell,
> The more we drink, the more's the flame in hell;
> Drink beer, to us by nature giv'n.
> When so inclined, you'll find the way to heav'n.

No-one ever produced more powerful expressions of the differences between the effects of beer and gin than the painter, William Hogarth. Gin Lane shows a city in collapse: everywhere buildings are tumbling and decaying through neglect, and only the gin shops and the pawnbrokers thrive. The citizens are shown as rioting, debauched, emaciated and beyond all hope: a woman smiles inanely as she sprawls on a staircase from which her screaming baby is falling to its death. It is a picture of total misery and despair. Beer Street goes to the opposite extreme. Everywhere is neat and spruce; new buildings are going up, trade prospers. The good citizens are not just plump, they are practically obese and an archetypal John Bull figure stands outside the tavern, a foaming tankard in one hand, a leg of beef in the other. The only building that shows neglect now is the once prosperous pawnbroker – the three brass balls are about to fall off the building, while across the street an artist is at work on a new inn sign. There is, however, a beery note even in Gin Lane. In the background is a steeple with, incongruously, a statue of George I perched on the very top. It was paid for by a brewer, William Hucks of Abingdon and caused a good deal of contemporary amusement.

> The King of Great Britain was reckoned before
> The "Head of the Church" by all Christian people;
> But his brewer has added still one title more
> To the rest, and has made him the "Head of the Steeple".

Were things really as bad as Hogarth suggests, and if they were what on earth had happened? Things were certainly very bad at the beginning of the eighteenth century when the death rate actually exceeded the birth rate, and contemporaries had no hesitation in laying the blame at the door of those politicians who had legislated to encourage the drinking of gin at the expense of ale and beer. These were the days when the famous signs appeared: "Drunk for a penny, Dead drunk tuppence". Why should something seen by so many as a great evil have been actively encouraged? As in so many political decisions, the answer can be found in the exchequer. Europe as a whole was going through something of a spirit craze with brandy in France and geneva in Holland and, as always in Britain, there was no shortage of voices raised to deplore foreign intrusion. Among them is that of John Taylor who thought about foreign wines and spirits much as he did about foreign hops and beer.

Thus Bacchus is ador'd and deified,
And we *Hispanialized* and *Frenchified*;
While *Noble Native Ale* and *Beere's* hard fate
Are like old Almanacks, quite out of date.

The government decided to go along with popular sentiment and encouraged local liquids whilst discouraging the import of foreign alternatives. This was not entirely a disinterested attitude.

The beginnings of this story lie in the English Civil War. Wars are expensive things to run and Parliament hit on the bright idea of a tax on luxuries, including beer. The Royalists, recognizing a good thing when they saw it, did the same. It is a curious thing about taxation, that a tax levied to meet a particular emergency seldom disappears when the emergency ends. In fact, when the war ended the tax went up not down and a new word entered the language – "excise" – a bit chopped off. It was not popular. Dr Johnson defined it in one of his more telling phrases as "a hateful tax levied upon commodities, and adjudged not by the common judges of property, but wretches hired by those to whom excise is paid". The smuggling fraternity showed their aversion to the tax in a decidedly practical manner, whilst in Scotland, the illicit stills thrived. It proved, however, very lucrative for the government, even though brewers grumbled and the quantities of ale brewed in the land began to decline. The taste for European spirits, however, posed a real threat to the revenue. The government, pleading patriotism, had a brilliant notion – make spirits at home.

Brewers were now licensed to make cheap gin. This had two main advantages to the government. It produced a high demand for home grown cereals – excellent news for the land owning politicians – and it helped to reduce the imports of foreign merchandise. The duty on beer went up and the duty on gin came down with disastrous results, especially in the cities. Anyone could sell gin. You had no need for inn or tavern, any shop would do and even a wheelbarrow in the street would serve. Between 1710 and 1740 the consumption of gin trebled and even Parliament eventually noticed that something had gone badly wrong. In 1751, another act was passed whopping a heavy tax on spirits and limiting the number of places that could sell the stuff. The worst of the gin epidemic was over, and Britain had acquired its licensing laws at the same time.

Beer now began to come into its own and it was, like the steam engine and the cotton mill, a creature of the Industrial Revolution. Improvements in transport in particular were to have a dramatic effect, for now beer could be brewed, poured into a barrel and sent all over the country, first on the new system of canals, then later by railway. The local industry was on its way to becoming a national industry and the first of the great names began to apper. The classic example of the successful new brand of brewers was that of Bass of Burton-on-Trent. The brewing of beer in Burton goes right back to the thirteenth century when the abbey dominated the little town. Legend has it that the abbot was both a good brewer and a somewhat crafty fellow:

The Abbot of Burton brewed good ale,
On Fridays when they fasted,
But the Abbot of Burton never tasted his own
As long as his neighbour's lasted.

The local ale had a special quality thanks to the local water which came not from the river but from wells. That water remains the most important factor in the success of the area, and so good is it that waters from other sources are treated with chemicals by those less fortunately placed to produce the same balance of salts – a process known as Burtonization. But to return to the town itself, and to jump forward a few centuries, we reach 1766 and the start of work on the Trent and Mersey Canal. This artificial waterway was known as the Grand Trunk, and grand it was for it joined the west coast to the east – and it passed close by Burton-on-Trent. Now goods could be moved with ease to rapidly growing towns such as Manchester or brought to the ports of the Mersey and the Humber. Burton's beers were soon finding themselves a very long way from home as hogsheads were shipped out to the Baltic states.

Among the many who mixed in a little brewing with other trades was a carrier, William Bass. His beer began to find favour with an ever widening circle of admirers, so he struck a deal with another carrier anxious to expand his business. The carrier was Pickford, who went on to become famous in his own field whilst Mr Bass set about his task of providing beer for the masses. He was a man who had arrived in the right trade, in the right place at the right time. For he started up a business as a full-time brewer in 1777, the year the Trent and Mersey Canal was completed. Mr Pickford's boats were soon kept busy carrying Mr Bass's beer, and as the canal system spread, so the trade spread with it to such an extent that Bass were able to maintain their own warehouse at Paddington Basin in London.

Improved transport systems do more than just move barrels of beer from one end of the country to the other – they help every sort of communication, including the communication of ideas. So when the Bar Brewery in London developed a new, light, sparkling beer with a distinctive bitter tang to it, Bass were soon trying the brew for themselves. Once again, the local waters proved ideal for the new beer and thanks to the communications with the ports, the brewers had the ideal customers. Out in the Far East in the midday sun, mad dogs strolled and Englishmen dreamed of home and beer. Empire building was thirsty work and soon ships of the East India Company were including pale ale in their cargo – East India Pale Ale they called it, later just I.P.A. For it was not just the sahibs and memsahibs who found the new drink to their taste, it proved just as popular nearer to home. It is said that the delectable liquid only reached the home market by accident. In 1827 a ship was wrecked in the Irish channel. On board was a cargo of 300 hogsheads of I.P.A., and those that could be salvaged were sold off in Liverpool. The gentlemen in solar topees' loss was the Liverpudlians' gain and the pale ale of Empire had found a new market.

The real boost to the Bass fortunes came with the building of the Midland Railway which reached Burton in 1839. Michael Bass was in charge in those days and he was an astute man. He was quick to see the potential gain. He became a director of the railway company and made sure things went the brewer's way so that for example when they came to build the cellars under St Pancras Station they were designed to hold Bass hogsheads. The result was that the brewery could triple its output over the next eight years. Bass, in fact, grew so rapidly and spread over such a large area that they finished up building their own private railway which by the 1920s had sixteen miles of track with the eight locomotives hauling waggons not only all over the brewery sites but across half the streets of Burton as well, which must have made movement in the town a mite frustrating. Not that people minded that much: the more the waggons rolled the more the money was coming in. And there was always the compensation of the Great Railway Excursion, when special trains collected at the brewery to take the whole staff off for a jaunt to the seaside. It was an operation on a scale that made the sending of an expeditionary force to Europe look quite a simple matter. At the other end of the railway scale was the splendid train consisting of a locomotive and a single coach which took directors and visiting dignitaries on tours of the works. The carriage and one of those locomotives is now preserved as part of the Bass Museum, but alas, has nowhere to go for the tracks were lifted long ago. A model in the excellent museum shows the whole set up as it was in its heyday, down to the most precise detail as though the life of the great brewery had been stopped for an instant, frozen, shrunk and put on display.

Success bred success and Bass began gobbling up its neighbours in a series of take-overs and mergers, culminating in the biggest merger of them all in 1967 when Bass Charrington was formed. The new giant was now brewing one fifth of the country's beer. What this all meant to the customer is something we shall be looking at a little later on, but one thing is clear: in two centuries the brewing of beer had been revolutionized and the revolution began very largely because a semi-literate millwright called James Brindley dug a narrow canal past Mr Bass's door.

Other great names came to prominence in the eighteenth century and remain prominent today. Young Samuel Whitbread came up to London from Bedfordshire in 1734 to be apprenticed to a brewer, and not many years went by before he had set up his own business at Chiswell Street. It was an area of literary rather than alcoholic associations, for Chiswell Street was named after the bookseller, Richard Chiswell, and next door was Milton Street, named after the poet who was buried in the church next to the brewery. Whitbread put up a fine, elaborate monument to the poet, but the inhabitants of Milton Street proffered less exotic memorials, for it was the great home of the hacks, better known to the world at large as Grub Street. None of this has got much to do with beer, unless of course one is trying to establish a system of values as A. E. Housman did:

Say, for what were hop-yards meant,
Or why was Burton built on Trent?
Oh many a peer of England brews
Livelier liquor than the Muse,
And malt does more than Milton can
To justify God's way to man.

Samuel Whitbread was, however, a man rather more interested in machines than muses, a true son of the Industrial Revolution. With a site by the Thames he had no need to turn to canals for transport but he did turn to the new engineers for other improvements. He went to John Smeaton, the designer of the Eddystone lighthouse, and hired him to design vast storage cisterns, the largest of which held 3,600 barrels of beer. But his greatest innovation was to bring in a steam engine from the most famous of manufacturers, Boulton and Watt. This "stupendous engine" was used for grinding the malt and to raise water for brewing. It was said to do the work of fifteen horses; not very powerful by today's standards but impressive enough in the 1780s to bring the entire royal family along for a look. The king showed a practical knowledge of the new technology and gave the queen and the princesses a half hour lecture on steam power: the commentator was too circumspect to record whether or not the lecture was accurate. One of the princesses, however, was keen enough to take notes and then remarked to her hostess, "I don't know whether you allow this in general, but you may depend upon it Mrs Whitbread I shan't set up a rival brewery". Then they all went off to inspect the vast cisterns. This was just the sort of thing to keep the satirists' pens busy. Peter Pindar, the pseudonym of Dr John Wolcot, wrote these lines on the fascinating information that the beer barrels in the vault would, if placed side by side, reach to Kew. How far, asked the king would they extend if placed end to end?

> To whom, with knitted calculating brow,
> The man of beer most solemnly did vow,
> Almost to Windsor that they would extend.
> On which the king, with wondering mien,
> Repeated it unto the wondering queen;
> On which, quick turning round his halted head,
> The brewer's horse with face astonished, neighed
> The brewer's dog, too, pawed a note of thunder,
> Rattled his chain, and wagged his tail for wonder.

The brewers were, understandably, proud of their achievement in bringing beer production into the new, vital industrial world – even if the old cottage brewers were, equally understandably, less enthusiastic. A pattern was being set that persists to this day, of big breweries distributing their beer over a wide area – but that does not mean that the beer they were dispensing was even remotely like that we enjoy today. For the great drink of the eighteenth century was not bitter, nor even mild, but porter.

You could almost say that the test of a good drink lies in the obscurity of its origins. It suggests that the origins are complex, which in turn indicates a complexity in the drink itself and all the very best drinks thrive on that complexity, on a subtle mixture of taste, colour and smell. Porter should, on that theory, have been a pretty good drink because no two authorities seem to be entirely in agreement on its origins. All, however, seem to agree that it began life as a mixture of different brews: where they disagree is over the precise nature of that mixture.

A popular drink in the early eighteenth century was an 'alf an' 'alf, a good old British compromise: half of the old fashioned ale and half of the new fangled beer. If you were not feeling particularly thirsty you could always ask for half a pint or 'alf an 'alf an' 'alf. Even more popular, it seems, was a three thread – a mixture of ale and beer as before to which was added a portion of tuppeny which seems to have been something like a brown ale. Other versions of the drink give different ingredients, but everyone agrees it was very popular with the customers, if somewhat less so with the landlord who had to visit three barrels in order to fill one glass. Then to his rescue came a London brewer, Ralph Harwood of Shoreditch, who found a way of producing a beer that would have all the properties of the three mixed threads. It became known as "entire" and – again the story is little more than rumour – when it proved to be especially popular with the porters in the London markets, Porter. Both names have slipped into obscurity, but neither has quite disappeared. You will still find pubs advertising "entire" in engraved glass, and a particularly fine sign carved on the front of a particularly enjoyable riverside pub, the Anchor in Abingdon.

Porter was amazingly popular in its day, and it was stored in huge vats. By 1802, Whitbreads were brewing 200,000 barrels a year and storing it in oak vats that could hold well over one hundred thousand gallons. A similar vat at the Meux Brewery, which stood 22 ft high, burst in October 1814 sending a flood of beer out into the Tottenham Court Road and eight people actually died in the great deluge. Happily, this was not a common occurrence, and porter remained a popular drink for a very long time. We can no longer know quite what it tasted like, but we can have a pretty good guess, for porter travelled across to Ireland where it was equally successful and where the success lingered.

The Irish brewers were not pleased by the arrival of competition, particularly as there was a decided advantage given to the

36

London product. Tax on the English beer was only a sixth of that on the local brew, and not surprisingly the Irish houses started to go out of business. An inquiry was set up in 1773 and one local brewer said he had set up in business about seventeen years before and things were now so bad that he was busily looking for premises in Caernarvon and Holyhead. He never found a home in Wales and when the Irish tax was eased he went on to brew a porter of his own which was to become famous throughout the world. The brewer was Arthur Guinness. It is incredible to think that Guinness might actually have been a Welsh beer, for surely there is no drink in the world more closely associated with a whole way of life than is Guinness with Ireland. An Irish bar without a row of half-filled pint pots waiting to be fed through the Guinness production line is as unthinkable as a Welsh Rugby club outing where nobody sings or a Scottish bar with no whisky. The bottled Guinness in particular with its deliciously biting tang is a drink of unique quality.

Guinness indeed is more than a mere drink, it is part of a whole Irish mythology. The pouring of a Guinness is a ritual to be undertaken with due solemnity; a slow, measured progress is essential to ensure that just the right amount of creamy speckled foam rests above the rich blackness of the drink below. I know that, scientifically speaking, there are no gradations of black: a thing is black or it isn't, but there still seems to be a richness to the colour of the Guinness drunk in one of those magnificent, ornate Dublin bars that appears to have a quality all of its own. And many a traveller in foreign parts has had his heart uplifted when he has spotted the familiar dark bottle with O'Neill's harp on the label, nestling among the pallid ranks of some lesser brews. And the drink you enjoy is probably not so very different from that which a wounded cavalry officer at the battle of Waterloo noted in his diary as being the principal factor in restoring him to health.

It is certainly the nearest thing you will find to the porter of the eighteenth century. The drink is now more popularly known as stout, a name which appeared in the late seventeenth century and got a mention in this poem by Jonathan Swift in 1720:

37

A poet starving in a garret
Conning old Topicks like a parrot
Invokes his mistress and his muse,
And stays at home for want of shoes,
Should but his muse descending drop
A slice of bread or mutton chop
Or kindly when his credit's out
Surprise him with a pint of stout

Pick any period and, it seems, you will find beer changing, and someone will be deploring the change. Take bottled beer, for example: no-one seems to know just how or when it was introduced. The best story gives the invention to Alexander Nowell, Dean of St Paul's, who went on a fishing trip up the Thames. The landlord of the Red Lion at Henley where he was staying, thoughtfully provided him with a gallon of ale to keep him company. He tucked his beer into the long, wet grass to keep it cool and set to work with rod and line. The combination of hot sun, no fish and a glass or three of ale had the inevitable effect and he slept the untroubled sleep that one would expect of so pious a gentleman. On waking, however, he found he had to hurry off and quite forgot the demijohn in the grass. But memory returned and a few days later he was back, and there he found his nearly full bottle. During his absence the still live beer had undergone a secondary fermentation and when he eased the stopper it shot out like the cork of a champagne bottle. The beer was cool, bright and sparkling. It is a good tale, and it is a shame that one can rarely savour bottled beer which still works in this way. Guinness is one – hence the care needed in pouring if you are not to get a glass of foam and no stout; Worthington White Shield is another, where equal care is needed to avoid filling the glass with sediment. Not that the sediment does you any harm – in fact it does a wonderful job in clearing out the innards – but it makes the drink look revolting, and a good beer should appeal to all the senses. I am fond of both beverages, great comforters when no real draught beer is available. Thomas Tryon writing on *The Way to Health, Long Life and Happiness* in 1691 was not the least impressed:

> It is a great Custom and general fashion nowadays to bottle Ale, but the same was never intended by any true Naturalist that understood the matter . . . all such Bottle Drinks are infected with a yeasty furious foaming matter, which no Barrel Ale is guilty of.

One of the latest importations to arouse the wrath of the patriotic suppers of the ales of old England – or as we should perhaps say the beers of old Holland – is lager. Now lager is a perfectly reasonable drink, made from the same constituents as our familiar beer but using a different yeast, known scientifically as *charomyces uvarum* (Carlsbergensis) which does not tell you a lot. The main difference lies in the way the yeast works. In making bitter, the yeast rises to the top of the vat, top yeast; whilst the lager yeast sinks to the bottom, bottom yeast. So not surprisingly, you get a different effect. At this stage, the good European brew is set to be "lagered", which means that it is kept in store whilst secondary fermentation occurs, just as in traditional beer, producing its own liveliness. We have the Americans to thank for the dubious privilege of enjoying, if that is the word, most modern "lagers" – the inverted commas are there not to indicate disapproval but because it is difficult to think of a non-lagered lager. Yet this is exactly what we get. Fermentation continues in the brewery until everything that should be fermented has been fermented, at which point it is chilled and carbonated. The result is a clear, bright, fizzy drink that you take cold and which fulfils the adman's dream – for if it is hard to imagine anyone liking it a lot, there is not a great deal to dislike a lot either. It is a bland product, frequently packaged under some exotic-sounding foreign name, though given the method used in production something transatlantic would be much more appropriate. Perhaps a name similar to that of one of the major American producers might be appropriate. Schlitz comes to mind, for it seems to convey much of the right feeling.

So we find the beer drinkers of the twentieth century campaigning for their traditional, home produced ale as vehemently as their counterparts did four hundred years ago – even if they are not campaigning for the same drink. Our quick flip through beer history has now brought us up to date and to another chapter.

3. On Every Infant's Tongue

O Beer! O Hodgson, Guinness, Allsopp, Bass!
Names that should be on every infant's tongue!
Shall days and months and years and centuries pass,
And still your merits be unrecked, unsung?
Oh! I have gazed into my foaming glass,
And wished that lyre could yet again be strung
Which once rang prophet-like through Greece, and taught
    her
Misguided sons that the best drink was water.

C. S. Calverley

Those lines were written just over a century ago; and of the four great breweries listed only two survive. Allsopp, after more than two centuries of independent existence, merged with Ind Coope in 1934. The fate of Hodgsons was even sadder. They were brewing at the very beginning of the seventeenth century, then they were taken over by Courage in 1943 and the brewery was knocked down in 1971. Now even the mighty Courage has fallen, taken over in its turn in 1986 by Elders, brewers of Fosters Lager. At the beginning of the century, there were almost two thousand breweries in Britain and those who have tears to shed and are prepared to shed them should look not at Caesar's corpse but at the corpses littering the history of British beer. Spend an afternoon with Norman Barber's comprehensive directory of breweries and their fates *Where Have All The Breweries Gone?* and if by the end the pages are not damp with salty drops, then you are no true lover of the foaming glass.

Diversity is not, however, yet dead in British brewing and in this section I am going to look at the British scene of today – and at the same time look at the whole business of turning a few simple ingredients into a drink that can be dully mediocre or magnificently satisfying. Essentially the quality of the beer depends as much on the quality of the ingredients as on the skill of

The Nine Elms Brewery, south-west London, built for Thorne Brothers Ltd in 1898 as featured in The Brewers' Journal *of that year.*

the brewer, and at the heart of the process is malt. We can take that back a stage further and say that the quality of the malt depends on the barley from which it is made. The crucial factor as far as brewers are concerned is the nitrogen content, and here the real aler meets the real farmer, for real ale brewing requires a low nitrogen content and it is the heavy use of artificial fertilizers which sends the nitrogen content upwards. The higher contents work well enough for keg beers and lagers, but tend to produce hazy, discoloured real ale. Perhaps this ought to be part of the campaign for real ale, a rallying cry for ecologists, though I am not sure that I can see a great future for organic beer. But that is what real ale thrives on, old fashioned organically farmed barley. It is, however, getting rarer.

The best results then come from the older style of farm and there is too an old style of malting, though you have to look long and hard to find it. These are known as "floor maltings" and the buildings are instantly recognized by their pyramidal roofs. Here the barley is spread out on the floor and soaked with water to start the process of germination. It is regularly turned with big flat wooden shovels to ensure a good supply of air and to stop the little rootlets entangling. At just the right moment, when the starch in the seed has all been converted to sugar, the process is stopped. The barley is taken to the kiln where the heat brings germination to a halt. This is an all-important part of the process, for the temperature of the kiln, the length of time the barley stops in the kiln and even the fuel used in the kiln will all affect the colour and flavour of the end product. In fact, to diverge slightly and turn to that other great British drink, malt whisky, it is the use of peat in the malting furnace that gives the very distinctive smokey taste to the whiskies of Islay. But, to return to our beer, the malting industry has changed a good deal in recent years, and if you look at just one old established company you can get some idea of the present state of the art.

In the nineteenth century, Mr George Paul started up a malting business at Ipswich. This was an ideal spot surrounded by the rich farming land of East Anglia and with a good port for shipping out the malt. They have expanded a good bit over the last hundred years and apart from their six maltings in eastern England they now have two in Scotland, interests in Europe and have even spread over to Nigeria. They still have a floor malting, even if it is not quite as it was in the old wooden shovel days. Nowadays automation rules and the turning of the malt is all done by machine. But this is still the method that seems to produce the malt that finds most favour with the brewers of the very best ales. At the opposite extreme is the new plant in Buckie on the east coast of Scotland which seems at first glance to have strayed across from Cape Canaveral, with gleaming alloy silos that look as if they might any day now shoot up into orbit. Here you have single vessel malting – which, as the name suggests, is one where everything is done in a single vessel. There are two of these vessels at Buckie each holding 550 tonnes of barley, and everything is controlled by micro-processors and computers. In this world of stainless steel and silicon chips it is a great comfort to know that the rule of thumb is still applied. The maltster tests the germinating barley by splitting open the grain with his thumbnail to reveal a white lump like a tiny piece of indiarubber. You can tell how far germination has gone by rubbing the lump between thumb and finger; when the process is complete the rubbery lump squashes down to leave a white smear. Science has yet to find a test that will match that of the good maltster's thumb, even in the most modern and sophisticated maltings in the world.

Although we are only just at the start of the preparations for brewing, now seems a good time to introduce the plant which once roused brewers and imbibers to such fury – the hop. It was not just prejudice: there was reason in the matter. Neither beer nor ale keeps for ever: a strong ale will keep longer because the strength of alcohol stops organisms attacking it; the hop performs the same function for beer. It was therefore argued that hopped ale could be made weaker and still be kept – and, of course, it would be cheaper to make. Would it be cheaper for the customer? You could give the answer to that at the end of the sixteenth century as confidently as you could for any similar magical formula at the end of the twentieth. This is the sixteenth-century view of Robert Greene:

And you, master brewer, that growe to be worth forty thousand pounds by your selling of soden water, what subtility have you in making your beare to spare the malt and put in more of the hop to make your drinke (be barly never so cheape) not a whit the stronger, yet never set a whit the more measure for money.

Hops won out, partly because the brewers found they did such a good job on the annual balance sheet, but also because the customers came to appreciate the flavour they give to beer.

Hops are grown in several areas, but far and away the most important counties are Kent and newly amalgamated Hereford and Worcester. These have remained the best areas for as long as hops have been grown in Britain, but change has come. The old varieties with such lovely names as Fuggles and Goldings are giving way to new with no less enticing titles, such as Wye Northdown and Bramling Cross. The new contain more of the resin that preserves and flavours than the old, but they have not quite removed the aged favourites, and part of the brewer's art lies in selecting just the right mixture to produce the best flavour. Changes in type are generally no more than a part of a general movement in agriculture to improve yields and to produce a "better" product – though that single word "better" could keep the experts arguing for a month. But another force is periodically found at work in the land: bureaucracy wants to get in its two-pennyworth or, in this case, two francs worth.

In continental Europe the growing of the hop has long been subject to regulations. The hop, like its growers, comes in two varieties, male and female. The female produces flowers whether there is a male around to fertilize them or not, and it is these flowers the brewers will use. For some reason, the Europeans prefer, nay demand, that their female hops keep their virginity. The male is banished completely from this vegetable harem. In Britain the male is permitted and even encouraged to flourish to spread his seed among the females. Here is a bureaucratically intolerable situation: different countries having different practices, a stain on the good name of EEC efficiency. Do the French wish to include the male in their hop fields? They do not. Do the British wish to banish him from theirs? They do not. Each country produces hops from which beer will be made to suit the individual palates of their nations. Is one method harmful? It is not. So why change it? No reason except for a desire to spread neatness, conformity and regularity in place of individuality, variety and choice. If rules had been approved as requested by the men of Brussels, the British would have been forced to conform. Inspectors would have been appointed to ensure they conformed, who would then have reported back to secretariats who could have reported to commissioners who could have told the legislators. And the Euro MPs in their Euro bars could have drunk their Euro beers happy in the knowledge that they had done their bit to turn us all into statistics. It has not happened yet but it is not for the want of trying. And where bureaucracy might fail, the accountants might yet succeed as they argue in favour of cheap, foreign imports. The traditional hop is everywhere under threat.

Even without these machinations, change has inevitably reached the hop fields. There was a time when the month of September saw a great exodus from the narrow, mean streets of London's East End as the hop pickers made their way to Kent. In the middle of the nineteenth century the pickers had to walk the whole way:

> The high road from London to the hopfields of Kent presents a curious appearance immediately before the hop-picking season. A stranger might imagine that the poorer classes of a big city were flying before an invading army . . . Towards evening the pickers cease their tramp, and take up their quarters for the night in woodland copse or under hedge-row or sheltering bank. Baskets, sacks, and hand carts are unpacked and here and there will be seen a whole family seated around a blazing wood fire, over which boils the family kettle.

The writer was not too impressed by the individuals who made up this army: "As a rule they are uncleanly, their habits coarse, their language foul and their morality doubtful." Not that the hop pickers gave a damn what anyone thought. For them the season was a chance to exchange gloom and soot for the open air and make a few bob into the bargain. Hard work it might be, but there was a festive air about the occasion that eased the labour and turned it into something like a holiday. It is a way of life that has all but gone. Once men on stilts cut down the plants from the high strung wires that laced the fields; now it can all be done from a high perch on the back of a tractor. Machines roam the fields where the Londoners worked in their thousands.

Once collected, the hops are dried in a kiln or oast house. The old circular building with its pointed cowl on the roof is as much a symbol of the Kentish hop field as the pagoda roof is of a Highland distillery. Modernization has brought change here and many of the old oast houses survive only as conversions, "homes of character" as the estate agents' jargon has it. But the essential job of growing and drying hops continues, and they are still sent off to the brewers in "pockets" – never in sacks. There they join the malt, the water and the yeast and we are ready to start brewing – but what a range of activities and places that simple phrase covers. So let us go on a mini tour of just a few of the different breweries, large and small, to get an idea of the varieties still to be found. We shall also take a nostalgic glance backwards to what once was.

There are certain brewing institutions which you might expect would have vanished for ever from the land. The great stately home might occasionally have preserved its brewhouse, but only as another exhibit to be perused from a distance just as the Chippendale chairs must never be sat on but only inspected from behind the red, tasselled rope that keeps the visitors in place. But, quite amazingly, the art of the brewer is not quite dead even in this rarified world, for at Traquair House not only do they still brew but they still produce an ale to bring a gleam to the connoisseur's eye. The house at Innerleithen can boast of being the oldest inhabited house in Scotland, for part at least dates right back to the tenth century. As early as 1107 it was a royal residence and twenty-seven monarchs have stayed under its roof at various times. Mary Queen of Scots stayed and tasted the local brew but, alas, did not leave a note of what she thought of it. Given such a royal connection it is scarcely astonishing to find that the laird was a devout supporter of Bonnie Prince Charlie. The prince came here, passed through the ornate gates flanked by great stone bears and advanced up the handsome avenue of trees to the great house. He was the last to do so, for after that the laird ordered that the gates would remain forever closed until a Stuart returned to the throne. At about the same time, they stopped brewing, which seems to be taking patriotism a little too far. Happily,the family decided to restore brewing in 1965 without waiting for a change in the monarchy. They produce a devastatingly strong House Ale and a scarcely less potent cask beer. The brewery itself has hardly changed since the time the new copper was installed at a grand cost of £8 back in 1739.

With a total output of less than 150 barrels a year Traquair House is scarcely a large scale brewer so this is perhaps the time to look at a commercial brewery. If we could step back in time, not so far as the Stuarts, but to the turn of the present century when the brewing scene displayed such variety, with virtually every area of the country supplied by its local brewery, what would we expect to find? What would the average, medium sized brewery be like? It is the sort of question you might expect to find answered in a museum such as the one in Stamford, once the All Saints Brewery. It is a lovely place to wander round, rich in atmosphere and with all kinds of fascinating items on display. But it no longer brews. Another museum is planned at the old Everards Brewery in the beer capital of Burton and here it is hoped to keep the place alive. They are in fact still brewing good ale in the traditional manner and are actively planning to turn the clock as far back as they can. At the time of writing, plans were well advanced for returning the original steam engine to the brewery and putting it back to work and already an impressive collection of artefacts and objects is being assembled. The eventual aim is to open it as The National Brewing Museum, but for the time being they can only take small parties by arrangement. But it is not actually necessary to go to a museum at all.

There are still breweries that have remained virtually unchanged for the last hundred years, and none can better exemplify the traditional Victorian brewery than Hook Norton which can be found in the village of the same name on the Oxfordshire-Gloucestershire border.

From the outside, the brewery presents a somewhat bizarre appearance, a sort of Tudor tower block – though the half-timbered bit turns out to be no more than a covered sack hoist. Tudor it is not, but tower it most certainly is, for this is a type known as a tower brewery. Everything starts at the top of the building and then gravity takes over the hard work after that, just as it did in the ancient brewhouse at Lacock Abbey. How does everything get up there? You find the answer to that as soon as you go inside, and you also discover what makes this one of my very favourite breweries, for there sits the source of power, the steam engine. This is no showpiece, but a machine that is used every single working day. Its first job is to pump the liquor, the water, up to a tank in the roof by driving a set of pumps as old as itself. After that, the engine is available for anything else that needs doing. You need a sack lifted? Very well, off we go: the engine turns, a belt whirls, the shafts spin and up goes the sack behind its mock Tudor casing. The barley needs milling – no problem, for the steam engine is a wonderfully versatile device. It is not kept on out of sentiment, but because this quite small, but very robust machine is simply too useful to throw away.

It we follow the raw materials up to the top of the building, we can then follow them down again as they go through the different processes that will turn them into beer. Up to the top have gone all those sacks of malt which have to be screened to get rid of rubbish such as small stones which sometimes get into the sacks. After that the malt is ground down in the mill. It is easy to get confused by technical terms and special nomenclature, simply because everything that goes into a brewing process seems to come out the other side with a new name. So malt goes into the mill and comes out as grist – hence the expression "all grist to his mill", for it matters not a jot to the miller what he puts in, for he will still call it grist when it comes out the other side. The malt is next mixed with hot liquor in the mash tun where it is stirred by the masher. At this stage, the mixture is known as "goods", the purpose being to extract the sugar which will eventually be fermented to produce alcohol. The end product here is called wort.

The next stage is to pass the wort on down to the coppers which are exactly what their name suggests, vast copper boilers. What the name does not tell you is what a splendid sight they make, for the metal glows richly over the curved flanks of the vessels. Here the wort is boiled up with hops and when that is all done it is passed through the hop back. Here the hops are filtered out, though there is rather more to it than that. The spent hops remove some of the protein that has come out of solution, which would prevent the beer ever clearing perfectly. The liquor now has to be cooled by passing through a heat exchanger – in other words the hot wort swaps some of its heat with cold water before passing down to the fermenting vessels. And here we must introduce an important body of men, Her Majesty's Inspectors of Customs and Excise, who demand to know the strength of the wort so that they can collect the appropriate taxes. The figure they use is one which can be seen on an increasingly large number of beer pump handles o.g. or original gravity. It is a number which gives rise to a certain amount of confusion so a little explanation might not come in amiss. If you take absolutely pure water and keep dissolving other things in it, then the more you dissolve the denser the water will become. So if you give your pure water a density of 1,000 units then compare the density of your wort with it, you get a measure of how much extra material has been added. The new figure is the o.g. which can vary from around 1030 to 1040 for your average beer, which means you have added thirty to forty units above your standard thousand for water, to Eldridge Pope's Thomas Hardy ale at a staggering – in more senses than one – 1125. Original gravity is *not* a measure of alcoholic content, though it is a very good guide to it. You could start with a low o.g. wort and keep the fermentation going until everything that could be converted to alcohol had been. You would end up with a high alcohol content, but precious little flavour. Alternatively, you could take a high o.g. wort and stop the process early on, which would leave a lot of sugar in the beer, making it syrupy and pretty unpleasant. The art of the brewer lies in stopping fermentation at the point where the liquid has achieved the perfect balance between alcohol and flavour. And that brings us to the next process.

The fermentation vessels are large containers where the liquid is brought to a temperature of around 60°F and into which the yeast is pitched: not thrown, not added, always pitched. For the next six days or so, the yeast will work away at the sugar in the wort breaking it down into alcohol and carbon dioxide. It is the gas that causes the mixture to bubble and foam up into a frothy head. If you stick your nose over a fermentation vessel the gas whips through the nostrils and clears them out at one sniff – though it is not, I believe, a recommended practice. When the brewer has decided that the mixture is just right, the liquid is run off, wort no longer for the great moment has arrived when it is now, officially, beer.

The final stage is to take the beer to be racked, that is fed into casks as draught beer. This is often spoken of as "live beer" and it is indeed just that. Yeast is not a chemical, but an organism, a living thing, and a secondary fermentation occurs in the cask. The beer will not keep for ever, and must be handled with the care appropriate to a living thing. Sometimes dry hops are added to the cask, and before leaving the brewery isinglass is added, an unlikely substance made from the swimbladder of the sturgeon. This is called "finings" and helps to clarify the beer. It does the job very well, but how on earth was it ever discovered? This seems to me to be far more mysterious than the discovery of brewing. What on earth made the man with the cloudy beer decide that the one thing that it needed was the swimbladder of a foreign fish?

By no means all beer is treated in the same way. Some is taken away for bottling, and in many breweries the beer is given a very different treatment. It is chilled and pasteurized, the second process killing off all the organisms that work on during secondary fermentation. The live beer is now dead and you can chuck barrels of it around and it will come to no harm. Equally, of course, it will not now be producing its own carbon dioxide. So, in order to make it bright and sparkling, gas has to be pumped in and you get a rather fizzy drink, produced in much the same way as you would make lemonade or soda water. This is keg beer as opposed to cask-conditioned beer.

There is no keg beer at Hook Norton, where beer is provided now just as it was at the end of the last century, and indeed you get the feeling that virtually nothing has changed here in a hundred years. Everything is of a piece here, from the sloping topped desks for the brewers and the panelled offices to the rich textures of wood and copper in the various vessels. Best of all are the cellars, as cool and mysterious as the crypt of an ancient church. It is a place to delight the senses – all the senses. It looks magnificent, the aromas of brewing seep everywhere, the textures range from the cool stones of the cellar to the warm woods of the mash tuns, a gentle hissing and throbbing announces that the steam engine is at work and last, but very definitely not least, at the end there is a fine beer to taste. That is what it is all about.

Hook Norton is an absolutely typical, medium-sized Victorian brewery where no-one talks very much about traditions for the very good reason that tradition is simply accepted without question. There are, thank Heavens, still breweries around where the same philosophy holds true. And even in those which have in recent years gone in for large scale modernizaton, a few remain who, while looking to the future, have not turned their backs on the past. This is a difficult posture to achieve, suggestive of a sort of temporal yoga exercise. It can be done, however, and one brewery that has done precisely that is Young's of London. In fact, going round their brewery in Wandsworth is a little like entering a science fiction time and space machine: open one door and you are staring at the bustling traffic of London's South Circular Road; turn to another and you are in the middle of an old fashioned farmyard. This air of unreality is compounded by finding that the brewery exists under the disapproving gaze of a Salvation Army citadel – though disapproval was temporarily suspended when the brewery celebrated three hundred years of beermaking with a visit from the Queen. Inevitably the passage of three hundred years has left marks on the old place.

It is almost impossible to give a coherent account of the brewery, for the generations have become muddled together over the years. It has not really been designed – it just happened, growing as demand grew, the new having to adapt to the spaces left by the old. The logical thing would have been to sweep out the old and bring in the new but that is not the Young's way. They have brought in new "coppers" in sparkling, silvery metal, but they have kept the old of 1869, bulbous and bright. They have held on to the malt mill, gleaming mahogany and brass, and, best of all, they have kept their two antique steam engines. They were both built by the local firm, Wentworth & Son, the first being installed just after the Young family acquired the place in 1831, but the second is a Johnny-come-lately of 1867. When I first visited the place in the 1970s they were both still earning their keep. This, alas, is no longer true but they are being saved – and they have earned a rest.

Young's like tradition and they have created a few of their own. No-one seems quite certain as to how so many animals got into the act. Horses, of course, have been there since the earliest days, hauling out the beer each morning for delivery to the local pubs. That is the job they still do, for they are economical to run and first class publicity. What can you think of that would give a greater sense of confidence in a traditional ale than the discovery that it was still delivered by horsedrawn dray? Then there is the name of the place, the Ram Brewery, which demands that you keep a smart, woolly coated beast in residence. The rest of the occupants, however, seem to owe their places to the horses. If you have horses, then you need an exercise yard and someone decided it looked a bit bare and dull. So a pond was put in the middle and what good is a pond without a few ducks and geese, not to mention the odd cockerel and peacock to keep them company? It makes the yard a jolly and unlikely spot, a bit of country in the centre of London, and what other justification does it need?

Those with an eye for history should take a close look at the exercise yard, for its edge is marked by stone blocks, each one of which has a hole drilled in it. These were stone sleepers into which

were spiked iron rails – stones rather than the familiar wooden
sleepers because they date back to the days when horses not steam
locomotives pulled the trucks and a clear pathway had to be left
between the rails for the horses to walk. These are, in fact,
left-overs from the Surrey Iron Railway, the first railway ever to
be approved by Act of Parliament, back in 1803. I imagine that the
occasional drop of Messrs. Young's amber fluid lubricated the
navvies as they toiled. Just as with Bass at Burton, Young's
thrived on its transport connections with a canal down to the
Thames, a connection still remembered by an old wharf-side pub
The Crane. If there is a better place to sample Young's beers then I
have yet to meet it. But the story always comes back to the horse:
horses pulling drays, horses pulling canal boats and even horses
hauling railway waggons, so inevitably all visits to Youngs
include a stop at the stable. There are working horses and show
horses here, twenty-two in all, and lording it over them is
Goliath, standing just over nineteen hands tall. My own acquaintance with Goliath was brief but memorable. "Watch it", said the
groom, "he's going to fart." And he did. If you can imagine sitting
in the middle of the brass section of a major symphony orchestra
playing the prelude to Act III of *Tannhäuser*, then you have got
some idea of the effect. It was a blast to shake the walls of Jericho
and one felt privileged to be present at such time.

Tradition and history then are everywhere present, but do not
have it all their own way. They have a new lager plant producing
what is reckoned by those who drink it to be a good brew of the
same strength as their bitters. But I must confess I turned back
with little reluctance to tradition. There are trades here that you
can scarcely believe still exist in the heart of London. There is a
full-time farrier, kept hard at it turning out horseshoes for the
great gentle beasts that need a new set every four weeks. And
there is a cooper – called aptly enough, Mr Wood. Now that
really is a craft that it is a joy to see preserved. Once every
brewery in the land had not one cooper but a whole department
of coopers. At the end of the last century, Bass had what
amounted to a whole factory employing four hundred men who
turned out over half a million casks a year. The metal cask has all

but driven the old wooden barrel out of sight, but enough survive to keep Young's cooperage busy.

The mystery of coopers as it was known in medieval times is a mystery indeed to most of us today, although the name "mystery" originally meant nothing more than a trade. But to us it seems a wonder when you try to think of the problems involved in making a curved, watertight container out of many individual planks of wood. It remains one of those crafts which have scarcely changed over the centuries, for it is the nature of the wood itself that determines how a cask is made. The timber, invariably oak, must be cut correctly on the grain and each separate stave carefully shaped so that all will fit together to make just the right size of vessel. The oaken cask itself has played an important role in the story of brewing and has brought outside influences to bear on the national drink. By Elizabethan times, there was scarcely enough oak to meet the needs of shipwrights and none left over for coopers, so it had to be imported from the Baltic. A brisk trade was set up, wood coming from Europe to make casks, many of which were in time sent back across the North Sea full of beer. It was a trade which did much to encourage the growth of the big commercial breweries. And in the names of the casks themselves we get reminders that it was the Dutch who first sent us hopped beer, and the terms they used for the containers, such as kilderkin and firkin are with us still. It is a pleasure to find a trade with such rich historical associations surviving amid the electronic controls of the modern brewery. History and tradition are here not thought to be incompatible with efficiency and modernity.

Someone recently suggested that it must be tedious visiting breweries up and down the country – a curious notion I thought, and one which rather goes with an under-valuation of the complexities and subtleties of beer. No-one ever seems to suggest that there is a limit to the number of vineyards you might wish to visit in Burgundy. Brewing still offers a world of almost infinite complexity and you could scarcely ask for a greater contrast than that between, say, the little brewery of Donnington housed in an old mill and crouched down under the lee of a Cotswold hill, and Batham's in the very heart of the Black Country. The settings could scarcely offer a greater contrast and nor could the pubs that they serve: country inns for one, town pubs for the other. And if anyone thinks that the first sounds idyllic and the other somewhat depressing, then I recommend a visit to The Vine next door to Batham's in Brierley Hill, as good an example of an honest, homely pub selling first class food and excellent ale as you would hope to find. But don't ask the locals where to find The Vine – for no-one ever uses the name. It is The Bull and Bladder to all and sundry and I have never been able to find out why. It might, however, be thought tedious to go through every brewery and even more tedious to describe each one in detail – though Alfred Barnard who visited every distillery in Britain and all the main breweries at the end of the last century has proved the contrary, for his books are still read with pleasure. I am not going to attempt that monumental task, but just try to give an impression of the range of activities, so let us have another look at the great beer town of Burton-on-Trent. Norman Barber's invaluable guide tells us that at the beginning of the century there were eighteen breweries in the town. Many have now disappeared, but not all – and it has not all been loss either.

At the top end of the scale, in terms of size, are the giants of the trade, Bass and Ind Coope, the latter part of the even larger Allied Breweries Group. We have already had a pretty good look at one of those giants, Bass, though it is worth repeating that anyone evenly faintly interested in the history of beer and brewing should visit the museum there. It does not just provide a guide to the main topics, for there are all sorts of enchanting things to be seen – a pre-war delivery van shaped like a beer bottle, a model brewery still occasionally worked by steam and a wide variety of objects associated with the trade. And once the second Burton museum is opened up at Everards, then no-one will be able to keep away from the town.

Burton still does boast one brewery which maintains a particular way of working for which the town was once famous and of which Bass had the grandest example, though it has been discontinued there. The brewery is Marston's and the system the Burton Union. Whilst working on this book I was constantly asking friends, acquaintances or just the toper propping up the other end of the bar which were their favourite beers. It was not, in any way, a scientifically conducted survey – and I have never made any attempt to do a serious analysis of the results. Two general trends did, however, emerge. Firstly, there was an obvious strong local preference, which partly at least depended on availability. Mention the name Timothy Taylor in Kent and you were likely to be met by as blank a look as you would get if you were to ask for a pint of Shepherd Neame in Keighley. But wherever I went, the name Marston's Pedigree was mentioned with relish, so that it was inevitable that I should make my way there at some stage or other, and the Union Room made the certainty doubly certain.

The brewery is, like Hook Norton, a very traditional place, full of old equipment, including a pair of century old malt mills and genuine copper coppers. That is all very interesting, but attention nowadays concentrates on the Union, the last of its kind still at work. This is where fermentation takes place, not in the conventional large vats but in individual barrels, row upon row of them stretched out in a huge, echoing room. As the process gets under way, froth rises and its only escape is through a swan-necked tube which deposits it in a trough above each row of barrels. Here the yeast is collected, and this is seen as the great advantage of the system as far as the brewer is concerned. The same strain of yeast can be kept going year after year after year guaranteeing the brewer will maintain the special quality and taste of his beer. That is the brewer's story, but talk to the engineer and you get a different tale. To him it is an old fashioned, inefficient and expensive way of brewing. Cleaning the system involves supplying 300 barrels of hot water every week. It is a nightmare of organization, for every barrel in the Union has to be kept full of liquid to keep the wood from shrinking. You cannot repair barrels in situ: if anything goes wrong the individual cask has to be removed and sent to the cooper for repair. The engineer reckons that doing away with the Union could save £3–4,000 a year. That is viewing it purely in his terms: and he is the first to admit that there is more to brewing than efficiency. What really counts and what keeps the customers paying for the product is the quality of the beer. As long as the brewer can convince the engineer that Pedigree wouldn't be Pedigree without the Union – then the old system is safe. And it was the engineer himself who told me the tale of a nationally famous brew where the plant was modernized in the 1960s – and the beer was never the same again. All the ingredients were the same and no-one could locate the point where it had gone wrong. They never did find the answer, proof indeed that there is as much art as science in the production of a fine ale.

The newest addition to the ranks of Burton breweries is the Burton Bridge Brewery which, naturally enough, is to be found at the end of the bridge over the Trent. It was only begun in 1982 but it has already achieved a good deal of success and acclaim. I first encountered the beer in a little pub in Derbyshire where I was eyeing quite an impressive array of hand pumps offering some excellent beers. It was the landlord who persuaded me to try the Burton Bridge declaring it to be the best beer he had ever tasted: praise indeed, and as it was by no means the most expensive on offer I assumed that it was disinterested advice. We sipped at the Bridge Bitter, quite strong by bitter standards with a very distinctive, round flavour. Whether it is the best in Britain or not I would not care to say. I do not in fact believe there is such a thing, for so many factors affect a tasting from the quality of the pub cellar to the mood of the day. But it was certainly a beer to savour and enjoy, a more than welcome addition to the long list of great beers from Burton.

The two founding fathers, Bruce Wilkinson and Geoff Mumford, were both well established as what one might call medium sized cogs in one of the larger brewery machines and could, no doubt, had they bided their time, eventually have become big cogs. But not everyone it seems is happy as a cog, no matter how large, and they dreamed of independence. The dreams might have remained separate and unrealized had they not happened to have worked the same night shift and discovered an ambition to run an independent brewery producing first class beer. It is easy enough to share a vision, but rather more difficult to turn it into reality.

They began investigating ways and means, and soon came to the conclusion that there was little point in starting a brewery without an outlet for the produce. What they needed, in short, was a pub with space to brew. They found what they wanted in Burton. It is bad enough starting up a new pub and a new brewery anywhere in Britain, but to start them in the brewery capital where all the citizens believe themselves to be experts, might seem to be asking for trouble. But they accepted the challenge: in fact they went even further and in their very first year entered their brew in the National Festival – and walked off with a prize. There is no great secret to success, just sound brewing principles, first class ingredients and a great deal of hard work. When you are boss of your own brewery, chances are that all the tough jobs fall on your own shoulders, literally. You have to hump the sacks of malt and the pockets of hops: you have to roll out your own barrels. A few more years have to go by before the degree of success can be measured, but the signs are good. The pub thrives, deservedly, and the beer is being sent out to an ever increasing number of pubs in the region. It is a small beginning – but then William Bass started off with very little more.

Burton Bridge represents a stage beyond the old style pub brewery, where everything that was produced by the local was sold to the locals. Once, this was the normal state of affairs: the alehouse keeper was also the brewer, but with the growth of the big companies the system died away and all but disappeared. When Michael Dunn wrote his *Guide to Real Draught Beer* in 1979 he could only list four old established home brew pubs and six newcomers, of whom half were more or less casual about their brewing. Less than a decade later, the CAMRA *Good Beer Guide* was listing seventy-six home brew pubs – not, one has to say, all brewing with equal success. I have been offered some strange opaque liquids whose only claim to fame seemed to be their undoubted laxative properties. Other home brews, however, have long histories and excellent qualities and one of the most famous of all is the Old Swan at Netherton, known through the area as Ma Pardoe's.

If anyone had been in the business of electing Pub Brew

Queens then the coronet would surely have gone each and every year right up to her recent death to Doris Pardoe. Hers was a name uttered with reverence, for she was upholder of a great tradition. The Pardoes came to the area in 1932 when it was still a commonplace to find pubs producing their own beer, and she lived on to find herself the Black Country's sole surviving publican-brewer. Now, the movement has gained fresh impetus but there are few places which can boast a true brew house of their own, an old purpose built establishment, a place that was built to last. The pub was never a pretentious place. The main thing that caught the eye when you walked in was the old black stove with a chimney that seemed to point in every direction except up. Now there is no Ma Pardoe but CAMRA are keeping the place going, and they at least are a body that realizes that this is something more than a pub with a brew house at the back. It is a survivor from an age that can never really return, for however much the publican brewer tries he or she is, to a large extent, trading on a novelty value. Doris Pardoe was running a plain pub in a plain area that just happened to sell her own plain beer, turned out as it had been for years by the brewer George Cooksey. Whatever it might be or become, it will never be just another Black Country boozer.

I have already described a few more breweries in this chapter and mentioned a few more, and I might have given the impression that Bacchus is in his Heaven and all's well with the world. But the second half of the twentieth century has seen great changes, changes which have threatened the survival of the traditional British pint. Now there is not necessarily anything wrong with that. Hopped beer destroyed the market for the genuine English ale and I for one would not wish to go back to the sweet, heavy drinks of old. Now we have seen the arrival of keg beer followed by lagers, and there is nothing in morality to say the newcomers are bad and real ale good. Are they not just another advance, a better product?

The answer is an unequivocal and resounding – no! What the keg beer did was to provide a consistent product, always clear, always bright and sparkling – but it is a sad fact of life that this sort of consistency is irreconcilable with individuality. A keg beer is a dead beer; there is quite simply no opportunity for it to develop subtlety and character, for that development is stopped at a crucial stage. It is undeniably convenient to handle but convenience is no substitute for quality. Just try and persuade a wine connoisseur that this year's Euro plonk is better than a fine old vintage claret because you don't have the bother of decanting it. Equally, lager can be a fine drink – but British lager is, in general, a pallid pretender, a poor weak creature when compared with its European cousin. I have no wish to prevent people drinking keg beer or lager: if it suits your taste, carry on and enjoy it and good luck to you. I would, however, contend that you are not getting the full experience, the total richness which a good beer can provide. And I do object most strenuously to the effort of some brewers to expand the sale of their convenience drinks at the expense of the real stuff. And here I have to put in a word for the organization that has done more than any other to ensure that there is still a real ale to fight for.

CAMRA first saw the light of day in 1969. It is not as its opponents sometimes claim, an organization founded to force everyone to drink real ale - even if on occasion one has met members who act as if it were. It had a quite different aim: to stop the big breweries forcing everyone to drink their keg beers and, to a lesser extent in those days, lager. The big companies were moving forward on two fronts. They were buying up small breweries, not to take advantage of their brewing capacities, not to preserve the special qualities of the brews they produced or anything of that nature. Once they had a brewery in their grasp they either closed it down or used it for storage. For it was not the breweries they wanted, but the tied houses. Out of the pubs went the local brews, the cask conditioned beers and the hand pumps; in came the new keg and the CO_2 cylinders. Then the second part of the campaign began: they sent out their advertising battalion to try to persuade the customers that this was what they had wanted all along.

The founders of CAMRA were convinced that they were not alone in wishing to see choice extended not annihilated. No-one can reasonably object to a new beer being brought in, even if it is not to one's taste – but they can object to the old, natural flavourful beer being shoved out to make way for the newcomer. The fight was on, and if any bookies had been taking bets they would probably have given you 10–1 on for the Big Six Brewers, 100–1 against CAMRA. It would have been a good bet to lay, for the amateur protesters took on the professional publicists and the wealthy businessmen and if they did not win outright they succeeded in halting and turning back the march of the kegs. When did you last hear anyone admit in public that they actually liked Red Barrel? The battle continues.

I had tended to believe that the contest was very much a modern affair until I read Lord Askwith's *British Taverns* published in 1928, a survey of the law relating to pubs and beer. There I discovered that this whole problem of big brewers taking over the industry was actually brought before Parliament and discussed by a special committee as long ago as 1818. This is what they had to say in their report:

> Committee were fully of opinion that so far from the larger brewers having, as was supposed, done a public injury by reason of what was called the monopoly of their trade, they had, on the contrary, done a public benefit by the superior article which it was ascertained they were enabled to furnish upon the better arrangement which their large and extensive capitals necessarily commanded.

The big brewers of today would no doubt heartily applaud. After all it sounds reasonable enough. Yes, but just look at the facts. Has the public been given a better service? Emphatically it has not. In spite of the so called "economies of scale" their beer is no cheaper than that of the small independents. It is often, in fact, a lot dearer. Is it a "superior article"? It is not, or at least not very often. Inevitably questions of quality come down to individual judgement, but those who are serious about beer would stead-fastly argue that traditional ales have a range and depth of flavour which is simply not possible in the chilled, pasteurized, gaseous alternatives. And this is a view which is about as much open to question as the view that a wine connoisseur is entitled to say that a bottle of vintage Bordeaux is better than a supermarket Moroccan red. This is not to say that all real ales are good, for that would be absurd. Some beers I find very far from being to my taste – and some beers which leave the brewery in prime condition are ruined by bad management in the pub cellar – not to mention sharp practices. I once knew a pub where it was a regular practice at the end of the day to empty all the slops into the draught mild. But what the real ale has is a potential for excellence: it can reach standards that other beers cannot reach, whatever the admen may say to the contrary. It will have true character and individuality. This, for me, is what the fight is all about: the preservation of choice and independence. I have not always agreed with CAMRA in the past. I have drunk beers they recommend in pubs they recommend and have liked neither beer nor pub. I often found members to be patronizing towards those who do not share their particular tastes. But Heaven help us, where would we be now without them? It does not bear thinking about.

The alehouse kitchen by Thomas Rowlandson.

4. Someone take me to a Pub

I know where Men can still be found,
Anger and clamorous accord,
And virtues growing from the ground,
And fellowship of bed and board,
And song, that is a sturdy cord,
And hope, that is a hardy shrub,
And goodness, that is God's last word –
Will someone take me to a pub?

G. K. Chesterton

Chesterton had a vision of a perfect pub, full of good fellowship and solid, traditional character. Many of us share the same dream of finding the perfect pub, but would ours be the same as Chesterton's? Probably not, for the pub has been constantly changing over the centuries and our own attitudes have changed as well. Today most people probably have not one but two ideal pubs in mind – one for the country and one for the town. The country pub will be all high settles and well scrubbed tables, a plain place where the beer comes straight from the barrel and the cheese comes straight from the farm. The town pub, on the other hand, is more likely to be a riotous mixture of plush seats, highly polished mahogany, shining zinc bars and cut glass mirrors. Different they may be, but neither ideal really belongs to our own age – they look back with a nostalgic glance to the pubs of a hundred years ago. Do our ideals really exist? Did they indeed ever exist at all?

If you look back over the history of the pub, you will find that our two ideals probably draw on two quite different traditions. There was the inn where the traveller could expect food, drink and a bed for the night. This is the building that still features on a million Christmas cards. Mine host stands at the doorway, through which one can see a merry crowd gathered round the fire. The mail coach is just leaving, with equally merry passengers perched on top waving their farewells. In reality, the crowd inside were probably mainly cheered by the thought that they did not have to suffer the horrors of the coach and the outside passengers just setting off were, to rephrase the poem, not waving but freezing. There are several accounts to be read of passengers quite literally freezing to death on mail coaches. Yet the scene persists, portraying a romantic past which is somehow better than our own dull present, In reality, only an idiot would exchange the heated motor car for the freezing stage coach.

The other tradition is of the ale house or tavern, neither of which offered accommodation. They were in fact slightly different, the tavern concentrating on wine and usually providing food, while the ale house doled out the beer. These are the forerunners of our town pub. Again, however, the popular taste now runs toward something from the end of the last century, the style which only fifty years ago was roundly rejected. Here is Thomas Burke, writing in 1936 of just the sort of place that nowadays is likely to be bursting at the seams with customers:

> The shabby-flash front, the grime and dull glitter of the interior, the dock-like compartments which screened the customer in one bar from customers in other bars, and even screened him, by an erection of moveable glass shutters, from the staff and almost made him, when asked for his order, plead Guilty.

Such places are, he is happy to report, being replaced by a "bright, wide-windowed, airy tavern-restaurant, with mural decorations by real artists". And that, fifty years later is just the sort of place the modern pub enthusiast avoids. It is a view not limited to the enthusiast. Just think of the name "New Inn": the chances are 100 to 1 against it having been new within living memory. It is much more likely to date from the end of the eighteenth century, a far off time when progress still seemed a good idea. The first thing a modern pub designer tries to do is to find a suitably aged theme to give the establishment "character". But whether the flavour-of-the-month pub will seem just as appealing in a few years time is quite a different matter. Those who would plead for their versions of the ideal might, should they live long enough, end up revising their original recommendations.

The inn was born out of travel. The true nomads carry whatever they need with them wherever they go, but the occasional traveller relies on others to produce bed and board. The first inns arrived with the first roads, and those most famous of road builders, the Romans, certainly supplied inns at regular intervals along the way. There were official inns (*mansiones*) which were set up primarily as staging posts for the mail carriers and visiting dignitaries. These were surprisingly similar to the inns that were to serve the mail coaches many centuries later. One says 'surprisingly' because somehow you do not expect a Roman *mansio* and a Georgian coaching inn to have much in common, but when you pause to think about the matter it seems a good deal less amazing, for both were answers to the same problem. They provided accommodation for visitors who arrived by carriage and on horseback. So we find both built around a courtyard, where it was easy to move between accommodation for the horses and accommodation for riders and passengers. The one thing the Roman visitor had which was a decided improvement over the facilities available to his Georgian counterpart was a luxurious bath house.

The road from *mansio* to coaching inn is not quite direct, for a great deal happened over the centuries. As far as inns are concerned, the Dark Ages remain obstinately dark, but we can pick up the story again in medieval times, when as with the history of beer we are soon led back to the church. The pilgrim was a very important figure among the comparatively small community of travellers. Most people seldom strayed beyond the bounds set by home and the nearest market, but the pilgrim would make quite long journeys to visit important shrines. All the great abbeys and monasteries were anxious to ensure that a comfortable rest was available at the end of the journey. This was not entirely disinterested charity, for the pilgrim would be expected to show his veneration of the shrine in terms that could be entered in the ecclesiastical balance sheets.

The abbey would expect to entertain the grandest visitors in their own building, but they were well aware that the less grand were not always less generous. So inns were provided for the travellers, some of which had chapels attached in which the visitor could give thanks for a safe arrival and pray for an equally safe return. The clink of coins in the holy platter was considered a great help in acquiring a sanctified insurance policy. Some of these inns remained long after their religious significance was lost. The Star at Alfriston in Sussex started life as a stopping place for visitors to the shrine of St Richard in Chichester. You would not be able to tell this from the carvings seen on the outside which have nothing to do with stars or St Richard. There is a rather mangy red lion and the saint is Michael, shown doing severe damage to an understandably aggrieved looking cockatrice. There is also, for no apparent reason, a gentleman idly gnawing at a length of rope. But the best known of these monastic motels is probably the George and Pilgrim in Glastonbury, a town almost as famous for its pilgrimages as Canterbury.

The problem with tracing the history of the inn is that only the extraordinary and the grand tend to survive, whilst thousands of humbler establishments fall down, get knocked down or simply stop being inns and become ordinary houses instead. In terms of almost everything except use, the country inn and the country house were virtually indistinguishable. In the plainer inn the guests were entertained in the kitchen whether they were paying for the privilege or family friends dropping in for a chat. Ale was brought in a jug, replenished from a barrel in the cellar; food was prepared for the guests just as it was for the family. It was this very sameness that provided the entire plot for Goldsmith's comedy *She Stoops To Conquer*, in which two gentlemen from London are hoodwinked into believing that the squire's house is an inn. It is said that it was based on an incident in Goldsmith's own life when as a young lad he was directed to the squire's home in Ardagh and told it too was an inn. Squire Featherstone played up to the joke, and it was only when the young man came to pay up the next day that he was told the truth. At least he did not do as Marlowe did in the play and attempt to seduce his host's daughter in the belief that she was a barmaid. It may all sound a little far-fetched, but just a few years ago I went to visit The Bird in Hand at Kent Green, near Stoke-on-Trent. I walked in to find myself, to my embarrassment, in a living room and staring at a lady who stood washing up in the kitchen. I began to apologize, but was ushered in. It was indeed the pub and the aproned lady took a jug and disappeared off down to the cellar to draw a quite superb pint of bitter. Even after that it was only the sight of a dartboard over the fireplace that finally reassured me that I was indeed on licensed premises and had not stumbled on some unusually benevolent local family. After that experience, I have always found *She Stoops To Conquer* a good deal more credible.

The inn, like beer, reached its finest hour with the improved communication systems of the Industrial Revolution. Better roads meant better and more regular coach services. It was the start of a whole new age when, for the first time, people began to travel for choice and not just from necessity. The coaching services needed to establish definite stages at which horses could be rested, fed and watered or changed for fresh teams. Passengers also required feeding and watering, if not changing, and they demanded high standards. The answer was the coaching inn, set down either in the middle of town or beside one of the new turnpike roads. The coaches had their regular stops, but there were still those who preferred to travel in their own carriages or, for longer journeys, used the post chaise, the Georgian equivalent of the hire car. Lists were published for their benefit, giving likely stopping places. Mr Clemishaw of the Angel Inn at Wetherby in Yorkshire, produced a list of inns, none more than twenty miles apart, along the way from London to Newcastle on the route of the Great North Road.

One survivor from this list has an intriguing history, the Haycock at Wansford in Cambridgeshire. The place can boast a fuller, odder title – Wansford-in-England, and that name also explains the name of the inn. It seems that a local drunk went to sleep on a haycock close to the banks of the Nene that flows through Wansford. The river was in flood, the waters rose and all the while the drunk slept on. He woke to find himself adrift on an expanse of water and shouted to the first person he saw on dry land to ask where he was. "Wansford" came the reply, a name that meant nothing to the inebriate, who demanded to know where Wansford was. "In England" replied his helpful informant, so Wansford-in-England it became. I would not, however, like to suggest that The Haycock still provides a resting place for local drunks. The inn itself was rebuilt from an earlier building of the seventeenth century and still carries memories of the past in its old courtyard with a brewhouse, and less convivial memories in its cock fighting loft.

Other survivors on Mr Clemishaw's list have seen other changes. The Bell at Barnby Moor has now become Ye Olde Bell. Of all the many silly ways of renaming a place this is surely the silliest. This "ye olde" stuff originated in a misreading of the, now defunct, Old English letter "thorn" which looks a little like "y" and was pronounced "th". It might be acceptable if the seventeenth-century innkeeper at The Bell had decided to celebrate its antiquity by calling it The Old Bell which he might have rendered in the spelling of his day as Ye Old but to use such language in the twentieth century is absurd. Why is it done? What happens all too often is that you get a large consortium taking over a perfectly decent old inn which displays its antiquity wherever you look. It is then modernized, and a genuine old atmosphere is replaced by plastic 'olde atmosphere' reinforced by phoney 'olde' language. I think I prefer Mr Clemishaw's plain Bell of the last century to Messrs. Trust House Forte's Ye Olde Bell of this.

Many of the coaching inns have stepped firmly away from the pubby world and settled for the grandeur of hotel status. There are still, however, the old, smaller inns that preserve their dual function of providing both refreshment and accommodation, with the former at least as important as the latter. For many, these represent a glorious ideal, and our image of the perfect wayside inn has not changed in its essentials for at least a hundred years. Take away the reference to horses and Charles Dickens speaks as ably for the modern traveller as for his Victorian counterpart:

How beautiful the landscape kindling in the light, and that luxuriant influence passing on like a celestial presence, brightening everything . . . Cornfields, hedge-rows, fences, homesteads, and clustered roofs, the steeple of the church, the stream, the water-mill, all sprang out of the gloomy darkness smiling. At such a time, one little roadside inn, snugly sheltered behind a great elm-tree with a rare seat for idlers encircling its capacious bole, addressed a cheerful front towards the traveller, as a house of entertainment ought, and tempted him with many mute but significant assurances of a comfortable welcome. The ruddy sign-board perched up in the tree, with its golden letters winking in the sun, ogled the passer-by, from among the green leaves, like a jolly face, and promised good cheer. The horse-trough, full of clear fresh water, and the ground below it sprinkled with droppings of fragrant hay, made every horse that passed prick up its ears. The crimson curtains in the lower rooms, and the pure white hangings in the little bed-chambers above, beckoned "Come in!" with every breath of air. Upon the bright green shutters there were golden legends about beer and ale, and neat wines, and good beds; and an affecting picture of a brown jug frothing over at the top. Upon the window-sills were flowering plants in bright red pots, which made a lively show against the white front of the house; and in the darkness of the doorway there were streaks of light which glanced off from the surface of bottles and tankards.

Are there inns still like this to be found? Were there ever inns like this to be found? It is the romantic ideal, the exile's dream of home. It may sometimes be found, but sadly the chances are that it will be packed to the doors by account executives from London, down on expenses. I do know one or two remote places which come pretty close – and I have absolutely no intention of revealing their names.

What happened to the inn in the twentieth century for it is obvious that our image is stuck firmly in the past? A changing world called for a different approach. The coaching inn had already given way to some extent before the advances of the railway hotel, but major changes appeared when the horse was supplanted by the internal combustion engine. A new type of inn appeared – the road house, where the cosy courtyard surrounded by galleries – a type preserved rather like a museum specimen at The George Inn in Southwark – gave way to a four square building set among acres of car park. This, in turn was followed by the motel: all very useful places no doubt and meeting the needs of modern travellers just as the coaching inn did its day. But will anyone ever come to love the roadhouse and the motel? Somehow I doubt it. But the advent of the motor car was not all bad news to the world of inns. Both The Bell and The Star became private houses in the railway age and it was only the age of the motor car that brought them back to life as inns.

This is not the whole story: for every inn that catered for the stagecoach or the even grander mailcoach, there were a dozen catering for a somewhat more mundane trade. The carriers who took goods all over the country gathered at specified inns on specified days. John Taylor listed all these London inns in his *Carriers Cosmographie* of 1637. Had I been living in those days and had I been shopping for furniture in London and wanted it brought back to Abingdon then I would have gone to the George in Bread Street on a Wednesday to arrange for my chairs to be sent on the next day. Naturally, carriers heading south from London congregated south of the Thames, and even the rather grand George in Southwark was the starting place for carriers heading for Guildford.

The story of the tavern and the alehouse is rather more complex for the nature of the old drinking house was very much dependent, firstly on the law of the land and secondly on the nature of society. The needs of travellers remain basically as they were in Roman times – food, rest, comfort and good cheer. The drinking establishment whether pub, tavern or alehouse has had to respond to changing fashions and changing drinks. Anyone who tries to thread a way back in time through this maze finds that the closer he gets to the origins, the more complex things become. What was the original tavern like? We know its origins in language, for it comes from the Latin *taberna* which means a hut or a booth, but can also mean an inn, which does not tell us a great deal. Was it a rather grand place or a drinking house where you could doss down if you were too far gone to leave or just a drinking house, plain and simple? We have a name but not much else, and whatever they were like they were purveyors of Roman wine rather than British ale. It is tempting to think of the Roman departure being followed by the Viking invasion which took over the old *taberni* and switched drinks. It is equally tempting to turn to Norse mythology with its great feasts of warrior gods being tended by the Valkyries – the ladies who get all the best tunes in Wagner – and to see them as the forerunners of the modern barmaid. But we really get on to firmer ground when we move forward to medieval times with its alehouses and ale-wives. We know much about them, partly because contemporaries wrote about them, but much more because the legislature began to take an interest. The reason why they showed this interest was explained, in somewhat different circumstances, by Michael Faraday. The great scientist was demonstrating the phenomenon of electricity to the Prime Minister of the day who, showing less than total enthusiasm for the affair, asked Faraday why he should be interested. "Because sir," replied the scientist, "one day you may wish to tax it". There is nothing like the prospect of revenue to rouse interest in a politician. So it proved here.

In fact, governments started getting into the act in Saxon times, when it was thought the people were definitely spending too much time drinking too much – and there were too many of them doing it as well. In those days communal drinking vessels were common, and King Edgar decreed that these should be marked off with pegs to set a limit on how far down the bowl each toper could sup. The pompous and overbearing could be encouraged to drink well beyond the peg that set his limit, and the now drunk and foolish man would have been brought down a peg or two. The alehouse was already regarded as having a lower status than the inn which offered food and accommodation or the tavern which at least offered food. These, it was felt, were providing the necessities of life: the common alehouse offered nothing but a little pleasure and the chance to forget for a while a life that was both short and brutish. Controls were introduced and authorities began to insist that the alehouses were licensed. It must have been quite a job keeping up with the rules. In twelfth-century London you needed a licence if your alehouse was built of wood, but you could trade away to your heart's content if it was made of stone. This was not as arbitrary a rule as it might seem, for this was a time when the wooden building was a real fire hazard – as the Great Fire was to prove. In James I's time, there was a rash of new laws and licences were sold off willy nilly. The licenser in chief was Sir Giles Mompasson who collected licence revenue for the state on an official four-for-you-one-for-me basis. But even this lucrative arrangement was not good enough for Sir Giles. This was an age which regarded corruption as an inevitable part of all officialdom, yet still found his greed too much to swallow. He was booted out, stripped of his knighthood and fined. This was good news for the honest landlords who had been overpaying on their licenses, and bad news for the owners of brothels and dens of thieves who had been kept in business by bribing His Majesty's noble representative. Other laws attempted to regulate the price of ale by tying it to the price of barley, but just as now there were wide differences between the price you could charge in the country and that you could ask for in town. Price setting was joined to attempts at quality control, and ale-conners or ale-tasters were brought in to see to this important matter.

The law was introduced in those days when all alehouses brewed their own supplies, and it was decreed that when a beer was considered ready for sale, a pole should be hung outside the door – the ale pole. The taster would then come along, sample the wares and declare them fit for sale or otherwise. This was a matter of such great importance that it was not unknown for the taster to be uncertain about his verdict. Being a conscientious fellow and loth either to pass an inferior brew or to penalize a worthier liquor, he was forced, reluctantly, to taste it all over again. He had no need of an official badge of office for he carried his own with him wherever he went, as a fourteenth-century poet tells us:

74

A nose he had that gam show
What liquor he loved I trow,
For he had before long seven yeare,
Been of the town the ale-conner.

There was no shortage of volunteers for this arduous task, but whether it was a consequence of the effects on the taster's noses or a desire to set out a more scientific method, the authorities changed the rules. Tasting was abandoned and, according to tradition, a bizarre ritual was put in its place. The conner arrived as before, but now arrayed in smart leather breeches. Ale was then poured onto the bench and into the puddle went the conner's leather clad backside. There he solemnly remained for a full half-hour without stirring – though it was a foolish innkeeper who did not offer a tankard of something to help him while away the time. At the end of the half-hour he prepared to rise. This was the moment of truth: would the breeches stick to the seat or would he rise as easily as a virtuous man from a church pew? If he rose untroubled then all was well: but if he stuck fast, then the sugar in the brew had not all been turned to alcohol. The brew had failed.

Some have questioned the validity of this story, and I have to confess that the earliest mention I have found in print came some eighty years ago, but that did give the story in the form of a quote from an earlier authority, sadly unspecified, and that authority claimed to have it from an even earlier source. It was, you might say, a story that was told to me by a man who had it from a man who . . . I like to think it is true just because the image of the conner solemnly sitting in his puddle of beer is so beautifully absurd. But whether the practice was as legend has it or not, the penalties for producing a bad brew were both real and dire. The ale-wife – for by tradition this was woman's work – went to the ducking stool, and the ale went down the drain. In Scotland, they were more frugal and gave the failed ale away to the poor who one can safely assume drank it without bothering to sit in it first.

Alehouses could be found throughout Britain, and in spite of the various licensing laws there were as many without a permit as had it, and authority was kept desperately busy trying to keep tabs on what was happening. So in *Articles of Direction Towards Alehouses* of 1607, local authorities were being issued with these instructions:

First, that in every parish, hamlet, township, there be perfect and true Certificate made, how many Alehouses, or victualling houses were the last day of February last past. And how many of them by licence, and how many not. And what persons in the places aforesaid keep any Innes, and how long the saide house or houses have been kept and used for Innes.

The directive went on to claim that this would bring order out of chaos, reduce the number of alehouses and eradicate unlicensed houses for ever. It failed on all three counts.

There is no doubt that the alehouse was a rumbustious sort of place with standards of hygiene that leave a great deal to be desired. Robert Raworth wrote a strange little book in 1635 on the subject of drunks, called *Philocothonista* in which he gave his drunks naval ranks. Those of a queasy disposition should turn to the next paragraph.

He that having over drunk himselfe, and utters his stomake in the next fellowes Bootes or Shoes, they call – Admirall of the Narrow Seas
He that pisseth under the Table to offend their Shoes or Stockings – Viz-Admirall
He that is first Flau'd in the company before the rest – Master of a Ship
. . . . . .
He that belcheth either backward or forward – Trumpeter

And he offers this advice to drinkers:

I temper three cups to the wise man: one
To preserve health (if it be drunke alone)
The next of love, and pleasure, both to keepe,

Firme and intire: A third to provoke sleepe;
These may the grave and discreete men carowse,
Yet each of them part sober to his house:
No more I doe allow, who these exceeds
In a fourth draught, brauls, and contention breeds;
Clamour a fift: A sixt to Lust invites,
And loose incontinence . . .

No wonder that a little later on one finds pamphleteers deploring
the spread of the places. Both following quotations are from the
eighteenth century:

Nothing can be more certainly known than the horrid
Effects of alehouses. They are Receptacles of Sots, and the
Scum of the Earth, who delight in decoying their Neigh-
bours.

Vice, profaneness, and immorality, in all their various
shapes, most frequently take their rise from small, and
almost imperceptible beginnings . . . to an unnecessary and
ill-timed assembling at a public house; and, unfortunately
the profits gained by the host increase according to the
intoxication of the guests.

Even the critics, however, recognized that there were degrees of
unlawfulness, and it was generally felt that a place that served
food was a better class of establishment than a mere beer shop. An
odd "tippling law" was brought in which made it an offence to
drink for more than one hour without ordering food. The mind
boggles at the idea of enforcing such a regulation. Just imagine a
landlord in a busy pub trying to keep track of each and every
customer to see exactly how long they have been there and who
had had a sandwich and who had not. It was not a great success.
For those who framed the law were confusing cause and effect. It
was not the fact that men ate that kept them sober, but rather that
sober men went to eat rather than drink. The best taverns were the
great social meeting places of the eighteenth century, in which the

drink on sale was a lubricant to good conversation rather than an end in itself. Dr Samuel Johnson, that great upholder of public virtue, was a regular visitor to and advocate of the tavern, as Boswell reported.

> We dined at an excellent inn at Chapel-house, where he expatiated on the felicity of England in its taverns and inns, and triumphed over the French for not having, in any perfection, the tavern life. 'There is no private house, (said he,) in which people can enjoy themselves so well, as at a capital tavern. Let there be ever so great plenty of good things, ever so much grandeur, ever so much elegance, ever so much desire that every body should be easy; in the nature of things it cannot be: there must always be some degree of care and anxiety. The master of the house is anxious to entertain his guests; the guests are anxious to be agreeable to him: and no man, but a very impudent dog indeed, can as freely command what is in another man's house, as if it were his own. Whereas, at a tavern, there is a general freedom from anxiety. You are sure you are welcome: and the more noise you make, the more trouble you give, the more good things you call for, the welcomer you are. No servants will attend you with the alacrity which waiters do, who are incited by the prospect of an immediate reward in proportion as they please. No, Sir; there is nothing which has yet been contrived by man, by which so much happiness is produced as by a good tavern or inn.'

Boswell, himself, also sought out a few places where he would not have cared nor dared to take his eminent friend. In his *London Journal* he records a meeting with a "monstrous big whore" in the Strand , and they went to a tavern together with, as far as Boswell was concerned, most unsatisfactory results:

> I had an opportunity tonight of observing the rascality of the waiters in these infamous sort of taverns. They connive with the whores, and do what they can to fleece the gentlemen.

78

The eighteenth century could offer, it seems, taverns for all tastes. Johnson looked for and found wine that "exhilarates my spirit, and prompts me to free conversation and interchange of discourse". Boswell found satisfaction for his "lewd humour" and "low street debauchery". You could take your pick. But whatever the evils of the alehouses, they were as nothing compared with the evils which arrived in Britain with the House of Orange and the Dutch taste for geneva or gin. We looked at the gin craze in Chapter Two, so there is no need to go over it again, but it is important because it was out of the gin–beer conflict that the familiar pub was born.

In 1830, Parliament passed the Beer House Act, also known as Billy's Beer Bill after King William IV, which allowed anyone at all to sell beer provided they paid a £2 excise fee. The same bill reduced the tax on beer. It brought cheer to the beer drinker and found its way into popular song.

> Come one and all, both great and small
> With voices loud and clear,
> And let us sing bless Billy the King
> Who bated the tax upon beer

New beer houses opened up at a phenomenal rate in both town and country. The village of Islip, near Oxford, is a quiet place on what is now a B road, but in the last century it lay on the main coaching route between London and Worcester. The locals reckoned that there would be no shortage of thirsty travellers passing that way, and soon there were over twenty houses offering beer. Today, two pubs are quite enough to meet the needs of locals and travellers alike.

It is still possible to work out which of the other old houses were once selling ale under Billy's Beer Bill. It was so easy to set up in business, that almost anyone it seems could do it and some of those who did prospered. A canal boatman on the Trent and Mersey decided to give up his boating life and sell ale out of a cottage next to the canal at Etruria. His old mates proved good customers and soon the cottage next door was bought as well and the two buildings were knocked together to provide ample space for thirsty boatmen. At first, the alehouse rooms were no more than an enlargement of the old cottage kitchen, but by the end of the nineteenth century a bar counter had been added to make it easier to serve drinks. The alehouse was now a respectable pub and it remained as a basic Victorian establishment, the Bridge Inn, until the next great transport revolution of the twentieth century. Road widening provided more space for the motorist but the old Bridge Inn went. With its passing, a tradition died, for the old place had remained in the same family from the day it opened to the day it closed.

Beer and the basic pub did not win a straight battle with the ubiquitous gin – and did not always deserve to do so, for the beer was often enough of a very poor quality. The home brew of the tiny ale house could be a horrid, murky beverage, while the big breweries were mistrusted:

> The brewer's a chemist, and that is quite clear,
> We soon find no hops have hopped into his beer;
> S'tead of malt he from drugs brews his porter and swipes:
> No wonder so oft that we all get the gripes.

That song, which has a decidedly contemporary feel to it, is one of the many ballads quoted in Roy Palmer's splendid collection *A Touch On The Times*. But it was not merely the quality of the booze that turned the customers away. In the cities, the alehouses were all too often dank, dark, evil places. Charles Dickens, who painted so many bright, cheery portraits of village inns also produced this dark image of the Three Cripples, haunt of Bill Sykes.

> The room was illuminated by two gas-lights; the glare of which was prevented by the barred shutters and closely-drawn curtains of faded red, from being visible outside. The ceiling was blackened, to prevent its colour from being injured by the flaring of the lamps; and the place was so full of dense tobacco smoke, that at first it was scarcely possible to discern anything more.

The country pub might go its own way, developing out of the back kitchen into the back bar, but in the town there was a need to attract customers, to provide something a good deal more alluring than the Three Cripples. The gin palace was bright, gaudy, noisy, vulgar and alluring – an Aladdin's Cave with a licence to sell liquor. The town pub that we now think of as in some way typical developed from a combination of these two traditions: they added the wholesome qualities of the alehouse and tavern to the undoubted glamour of the gin palace. And if you want to pick on just one building that epitomized the new trend, then look to the 1840s and Islington in London. The Eagle had everything, and its adverts laid out a list of delights that could meet every need:

> the pleasure grounds, the collection of statuary, the garden orchestra, the fountains, the gas devices, the brilliant illu-minations of variegated lamps, in stars, wreaths and mottoes; the beautiful painted cosmoramas, the set scenes in the grounds, the magic mirrors, the Olympia Temple, the Saloon, the double band, the great French rope dancers . . .

And so the list went on, cataloguing the delights but coyly omitting any mention of alcoholic beverages. But what an extravaganza! What splendour! No wonder it attracted the small business men, the rag trade merchants who crowded round the Angel. No wonder either that the sweat shop tailors were prepared to pawn their special irons – their weazels – to pay for a night out. And so the Eagle off the City Road, and its clientele, came to be immortalized in rhyme.

> Up and down the City Road
> In and out the Eagle.
> That's the way the money goes
> Pop goes the weazel!

There was never to be another pub that could match its flamboyance, but there were many who tried. They set a vogue for cut glass that would bring brilliance to a dull bar, for fine woods, either real or produced by the grainer's art and for entertainment that would appeal to the great mass of the people. The Eagle was to be parent both to the ornate Victorian pub and to the exuberant Victorian music hall.

The new style of pub offered a full range of drinks to the customers. It was no longer necessary to go to a gin palace for hard liquor and to the ale house for a pint. You could get them both in the same place, and the wares were set out in new, enticing displays. Brightly coloured ceramic and glass jars held the spirits and they could be displayed on shelves, reflected over and over again by mirrors set behind that other new institution of the age – the bar. The old kitchen image had gone from the town pub, and even the wooden barrel soon disappeared from view as the beer engine was introduced to pump the ale up from the cellar to a tap behind the bar. The familiar pump handles which gladden the heart of the modern beer enthusiast had arrived. More than one engineer came up with designs, but one deserves a special mention – for he thought of all the drinker's needs. Joseph Bramah built the first recorded beer pump, which was said to be an "elegant" machine and was in general use as early as 1829. It was not much like the modern hand pumped beer engine, and was in fact a very early hydraulic machine – and any technocrats among the readers would find it a most intriguing device. But that is not the end of the Bramah story for, as the old pub graffito has it, "you don't buy beer – you only rent it". What goes in will eventually demand to come out. And, with a most satisfying sense of completeness, Mr Bramah also invented a water closet. Those who wish to know what life was like before the W.C. should head for Hampshire, to the village of Redenham and then locate the Dog and Gun. Behind the pub is a thatched privy with a two-seater thunderbox, which has the distinction of being one of only two Grade II listed pub loos. The other is the gents in the Philharmonic in Liverpool which brings us back to the Victorian fashion for splendid decoration and the richest of rich materials. These marble halls may not be dwelt in for long, but they are as grand as any described in the popular song – and the second line could be equally appropriate:

I dreamed I dwelt in marble halls,
With vassels and serfs at my side.

Love of show and finery were not the only distinctive features of
the Victorian town pub. It was also a place of seemingly infinite
small divisions which corresponded with the class divisions of
Victorian society. The pub was never quite respectable: so the
employer was as anxious to avoid the clerk as the clerk was to
keep out of sight of the employer, and neither wished to be seen
by the hall porter. So a special building developed: gaudy enough
to appeal to all, but carefully divided. Compartments led off a
central bar, each screened from the next by a high wood or ornate
glass partition. Once you could find these all over London, but
few survive – one notable exception being the Barley Mow in
Dorset Street. Privacy could be taken even further. "Snob
screens" cut off the customer from the bar staff. These swivelling
glass screens could be moved to one side to allow an order to be
given, but if kept closed then all the customer and the staff saw of
each other was an anonymous stretch of body between neck and
waistline. A few of these still survive as well, as in The Lamb in
Lamb's Conduit Street, though some of that pub's old secretive,
intimate atmosphere has been dissipated in recent years.

What you can still find in some abundance is the extravagance
of decoration, combined with friendly intimacy of atmosphere
that characterizes the best Victorian survivors. Here I would
suggest a move out from the capital to the provinces. The city
which probably boasts the finest selection of all is Liverpool, but
other places can claim individual pubs or rare quality. As a
student, I frequented Whitelock's in Leeds, Edwardian rather
than Victorian, but with a wonderfully rich, glowing interior. But
if you really want to capture the riotous decoration of the last
century, then you should cross the Irish Sea. Half the bars of
Dublin seem to retain this atmosphere, but if I could only select
one pub for demonstration purposes, then I should have to move
north to Belfast and the gorgeous Crown Liquor Saloon. From
tiled floor to ornate ceiling there is not an inch of the place that is
not alive with colour and decoration – all reflected over again in

the brilliance of cut and engraved glass. It is the sort of place you love or hate, but towards which you can hardly remain indifferent. In it the Victorian ideal of the people's pleasure palace had its finest hour. But having reached a summit, where do you go from there?

The sad truth is that our own age has made precious few positive contributions to pub development. There are many reasons, but to a large extent it comes down to a fragmentation of popular entertainment. The old Eagle provided all kinds of entertainment all the time. Gradually, however, things began to come apart. Amusement on a grand scale moved out of the pub and into the specially built music halls – though the music hall artists remained true to their roots. They were great patrons of the pub next door, and many finished up in the business as landlords and landladies. But the greatest change came with the First World War. The Defence of the Realm Act set strict limits on opening hours in order to keep munitions workers, soldiers and other potential drunks on the straight and narrow. It was an emergency measure designed to fit an emergency situation – and it has remained with us, more or less intact, ever since. Happily, one aspect at least has vanished from the statute books. The act made it illegal to treat a fellow drinker – no-one was allowed to stand a round. Admittedly there have been occasions when I have been caught at the bar just as everyone I have ever known seemed to walk through the pub door, and then I might have wished that the old law had never been repealed. But it had to go, for it worked against the very essence of the pub appear. For the pub is nothing if it is not social and sociable.

The Victorian age gave us two models of widely differing charms. It gave us the village inn: a place of comfort, good solid country fare and plain, old fashioned values. It was, at its best, quite literally a home from home. Look around any country pub that is described in the guide books as attractive, genuine, homely or whatever and you will find that it has something in it of that old farmhouse kitchen tradition of plain tables, wooden settles and gleaming brasses out of which it was born. People relax with the happy thought that they are partaking of a great tradition of the countryside – and if their view of the past is coloured by a false romanticism, then it is perhaps forgiveable. Rural life in Victoria's reign was harsh and unkind, but it was at least a life with a direct connection to a natural world. And at least you could be sure that your beer was made of barley, yeast and water and not a cocktail of chemicals. The ideal probably never really existed but we should like to think that it did.

The stolidity can be set against the glamour of the town, and the town pub laid it on with a vengeance. Austerity was not a word that featured in the pub architect's vocabulary. In fact, the appeal of the town pub lay in good measure in its being exactly the opposite of its country counterpart. Where, in imagination we see the yokels round the fire discussing the price of corn in the one, we can imagine the intrigues of city gents and chorus girls in the screened off cubicles of the other. Neither stereotype has much to do with reality, but then a good part of the appeal of the pub lies in a very different direction. Customers go there to escape the banality and dreariness of the working world. And today that escape lies mainly in nostalgia, which leaves us without any real notion of where the pub ought to go from here. The alternatives to the nineteenth-century originals – the smart art deco cocktail bars of the inter-war years, the echoing roadhouses of the motor age – have never really caught the popular imagination. So, for the time being at least, we look to the past for our ideal pub. Change will no doubt come eventually, but one thing will surely remain constant. Whatever the shape of building, whatever the drink on sale, success will surely depend to a very large extent on the man or woman who stands behind the bar.

5. The Warmest Welcome

Whoe'er has travell'd life's dull round,
Where'er his stages may have been,
May sigh to think he still has found
The warmest welcome, at an inn.
William Shenstone

Those verses, quoted with approval by Dr Johnson, may be slightly wistful about life but represent a fine unsolicited testimonial to the friendliness of the good pub. And that comes down eventually to the personality of whoever is in charge. Just as there is a popular image of the ideal pub, so too there is a mental picture of the ideal publican. He or she – and which you choose depends very much on the period of history, for both have been prominent at times – is plump if not downright fat, jolly, good humoured, talkative, yet able to keep silence at appropriate times, discreet and, above all, tolerant. The innkeeper is a paragon, not of virtues for there is always a slight edge of disrespect to authority shown, by the pint pulled after hours and a general distaste for rules and regulations, but a paragon of common sense.

It can seem to the outsider to be an idyllic existence. We pay for the privilege of going to the pub, but the landlord actually receives money to be there all day. Incidentally, from now on I am going to use "landlord" for both sexes simply because it would be boring to write "landlord or landlady" each time, and I am not about to coin a new name – no "land person" here. From our side of the bar, then, we see this jolly person, happily accepting a drink from a customer, chatting away to his friends and not looking as if life is other than totally delightful. No wonder you hear customers saying that they are going to pack in work, retire and take a pub. Next time you hear the phrase – take a look at the landlord's face. The quivering of the lips shows the degree of masterly self control he is exercising to stop himself laughing out loud – or bursting into tears. This chapter is devoted to the life and times of the innkeeper, landlord, landlady or whatever other name you care to apply to the one who is ultimately responsible for the character of your local.

The medieval tavern was presided over by the ale-wife or, more rarely, her male equivalent, the ale-draper. The barmaid, in popular fiction, has become a rather sexy character – not exactly a shy, demure creature but one of big personality and ample charms. The ale-wife has had a somewhat less happy press. The first author to paint a full portrait of the lady was the poet, John Skelton, who at the end of the fifteenth century was writing charming verses to various ladies of his acquaintance:

> With solace and gladness,
> Much mirth and no madness,
> All good and no badness;
> So joyously,
> So maidenly,
> So womanly,
> Her demeaning.

That is the sort of thing you find in most anthologies. But when he came to describing the ale-wife his tongue took on a rougher note:

> Her lothely lere
> Is nothynge clere,
> But ugly of chere,
> Droopy and drowsy,
> Scurvy and lowsy;
> Her face all bowsy,
> Comely crynklyd,
> Lyke a rost pygges eare
> Brysteled with here.

For those who find difficulty with his English, I can tell you that Skelton was saying that she looked ugly, was scurvy, lousy, wrinkled and as hairy as a roast pig's ear – which is scarcely chivalrous. The lady in question, Eleanor Rummyng of Leather-head, could hardly be thought of as a lure to her ale-house, but she had one saving grace: she brewed good ale. And that was considered a great virtue in a woman. In the sixteenth-century play *Ralph Roister Doister* two splendidly named characters, Tibbet Talkapace and Madge Mumblecrust, discuss a third, Custance, whose ale is well thought of, with her suitor Ralph.

Tibbet: Soft fire maketh sweet malt, good Madge Mumblecrust.
Madge: And sweet malt maketh jolly good ale for the nones.
Tibbet: Which will slide down the lane without any bones. Old brown bread crusts must have good mumbling. But good ale down your throat hath good easy tumbling.
Ralph: The jolliest wench that e'er I heard, little mouse, May I not rejoice that she shall dwell in my house.

It seems that there was, after all, only one true test for an ale-wife. She could be ugly, bad-tempered and so disagreeable that she might earn the old nickname of "Mother Louse", but if her ale was good all else was forgiven. The ale-wife achieved immortality, however, a little later on with Shakespeare's Mistress Quickly, the queen of all ale-wives and all tavern hostesses. In the two parts of *Henry IV* you have as complete a picture as you could wish of the boisterous, noisy, throbbing life of the Elizabethan tavern. Those who went there were not perhaps the most sober, the most serious or even the most honest of citizens, but life in The Boar's Head in Eastcheap sounds a lot more fun than that of the constantly intriguing, ever quarrelling court.

On the male side of the line, the innkeeper has fared somewhat better. It was, after all, the landlord of the Tabard who persuaded the Canterbury Pilgrims to tell their tales. But no matter how jolly the landlord, his establishment would, like that of the ale-wife, ultimately be judged by the beer he kept. The landlord was as aware of this as any of his customers. He was proud of his brew and keen to extol its virtues – with, no doubt, a small degree of exaggeration. The innkeeper Boniface of Lichfield, as portrayed in the restoration comedy *The Beaux' Stratagem* was not only an enthusiast for his own ale, but quite willing to demonstrate his enthusiasm in action. Here he is greeting his guest Aimwell:

Aimwell: I have heard your town of Lichfield much famed for ale; I think I'll taste that.

Boniface: Sir, I have now in my cellar ten tun of the best ale in Staffordshire; 'tis smooth as oil, sweet as milk, clear as amber, and strong as brandy; and will be just fourteen year old the fifth day of next March, old style.

Aimwell: You're very exact, I find, in the age of your ale.

Boniface: As punctual, sir, as I am in the age of my children. I'll show you such ale! Here, tapster (*enter* TAPSTER), broach number 1706, as the saying is. Sir, you shall taste my *Anno Domini*. I have lived in Lichfield, man and boy, above eight-and-fifty years, and, I believe, have not consumed eight-and-fifty ounces of meat.

Aimwell: At a meal, you mean, if one may guess your sense by your bulk.

Boniface: Not in my life, sir: I have fed purely upon ale; I have eat my ale, drank my ale, and I always sleep upon ale.
Enter TAPSTER *with a bottle and glasses, and exit*
Now, Sir, you shall see! (*Filling a glass.*) Your worship's health. (*Drinks.*) Ha! delicious, delicious! fancy it burgundy, only fancy it, and 'tis worth ten shillings a quart.

Aimwell (*drinks*): 'Tis confounded strong!

Boniface: Strong! it must be so, or how should we be strong that drink it?

90

Aimwell: And have you lived so long upon this ale, landlord?

Boniface: Eight-and-fifty years, upon my credit, sir – but it willed my wife, poor woman, as the saying is.

Aimwell: How came that to pass?

Boniface: I don't know how, sir; she would not let the ale take its natural course, sir; she was for qualifying it every now and then with a dram, as the saying is; and an honest gentleman that came this way from Ireland, made her a present of a dozen bottles of usquebaugh – but the poor woman was never well after: but, howe'er, I was obliged to the gentleman, you know.

A dreadful lesson indeed on the dangers of mixing drinks; though you will never convince a Scotsman.

You can trace the same character in literature right up to the present day, and the qualities that made for a successful innkeeper in Shakespeare's day are little different from those that will breed the same success now. We like to see our landlords fit and hearty and enjoying their ale: for if they don't enjoy it why should we, and if they look grey and glum why should we expect to feel any better? Old Boniface knew he was his own best advertisement. What strikes you particularly in looking over the old stories and tales is not how different things were in the past, but just how little they have changed. For example, we have surely all at some time or another had a favourite haunt and then found it changing hands: the old landlord went and a new appeared. Everything else changed as well. There is no reason, in logic, why things should not be better for the change, but somehow it seems they never are. Which is exactly what two carriers found to be the case at an inn in Rochester described in Shakespeare's *Henry IV Part I*.

Second carrier: Peas and beans are as dank here as a dog, and that is the next way to give poor jades the bots; this house is turned upside down since Robin Ostler died.

First carrier: Poor fellow! never joyed since the price of oats rose; it was the death of him.

Second carrier: I think this be the most villanous house in all London road for fleas: I am stung like a tench.

First carrier: Like a tench! by the mass, there is ne'er a king christen could be better bit than I have been since the first cock.

Second carrier: Why, they will allow us ne'er a jordan, and then we leak in the chimney.

And if you have never heard the word "jordan" used before, then I doubt if you will have much difficulty in working it out for yourself.

It is not only the proprietor who sets the atmosphere. In the false grandeur of the Victorian gin palace, the staff acted, it seems, as if it were a palace indeed and the bolder customers took their cue from them. Dickens, inevitably, has left a remarkable portrait in his *Sketches by Boz*.

The two old washerwomen, who are seated on the little bench to the left of the bar, are rather overcome by the head-dresses and haughty demeanour of the young ladies who officiate. They receive their half-quartern of gin and peppermint, with considerable deference, prefacing a request for "one of them soft biscuits," with a "Just be good enough, ma'am." They are quite astonished at the impudent air of the young fellow in a brown coat and bright buttons, who, ushering in his two companions, and walking up to the bar in as careless a manner as if he had been used to green and gold ornaments all his life, winks at one of the young ladies with singular coolness, and calls for a "kervorten and a three-out-glass," just as if the place were his own. "Gin for you, sir?" says the young lady when she has drawn it carefully looking every way but the right one, to show that the wink had no effect upon her. "For me, Mary, my dear," replies the gentleman in brown. "My name an't Mary as it

92

happens," says the young girl, rather relaxing as she delivers the change. "Well, if it an't, it ought to be," responds the irresistible one; "all the Marys as ever *I* see, was handsome gals." Here the young lady, not precisely remembering how blushes are managed in such cases, abruptly ends the flirtation by addressing the female in the faded feathers who has just entered, and who, after stating explicitly, to prevent any subsequent misunderstanding, that "this gentleman pays," calls for "a glass of port wine and a bit of sugar."

There were fine gradations in the Victorian pub, which were reflected in everything that went on – and everyone had a job and a place as strictly regulated as the below stairs hierarchy of a country house. Pot boys kept to the spit and sawdust of the public bar, whilst the barmaids tended the more genteel world of the snugs and private bars. The barmaid was expected to be bright, jolly and attractive – not an easy task when you are on your feet day and night. But somehow they achieved it, and though it is commonplace to read criticisms of landlords, no-one ever seemed to have a bad word for the barmaid. Now, however, she appears to be a dying breed. I met the genuine article, quite recently, in a pub in Plymouth. She had a bosom that defied the laws of gravity and appeared about to make an escape to start a separate existence. The hairstyle was pure baroque, a piled-up confection of whirls and curls that would have made an admirable centre-piece for a Victorian dinner table. She had the warmth and friendliness that one thought only existed in pub mythology – and to top it all, she boasted a pure, rich Devonian accent. " 'Ere you are my lover", she said, as she handed over a pint and some of the best crab I have tasted in years. It was worth visiting the pub just to meet such a fine lady. Did barmaids always conform to a stereotype? Well, according to T. E. B. Clarke, writing in 1938: "Most barmaids are called Ruby, and they usually come from Portsmouth. It is hard to say why." Indeed it is. It would be equally hard to test the theory, but it would be interesting to try. When the last barmaid has drawn the last pint, then a certain brightness will have gone out of pub life.

Landlords or innkeepers certainly cannot be put into neat categories. They come from all walks of life and all social classes – and should be prepared to cope with all walks of life and all social classes. Even the most fastidious of innkeepers is still a person with a public house. John Fothergill kept The Spreadeagle Inn at Thame in the 1920s, and encouraged "nice people" whilst discouraging the far more extensive group of the less than nice. That group was headed by farmers and commercial travellers, of whom he disapproved. Yet even he surely speaks for all innkeepers in this description:

> Perhaps indeed this most inclusive and interesting of all trades or professions gives you the chance, if you have it in you, of filling a more varied role than any other, and, in return, of liking more people and in more different ways. . . . Doctors, lawyers and accountants are visited for temporary ailments and needs, priests and county folk only in morbid circumstances, but Innkeepers for eating, drinking, talking, relaxation, sleeping and all that's good.

It does sound rather attractive, doesn't it? Which brings us back to that popular dream of retiring to a quaint, old thatched pub in an idyllic village to play the role of mine host. There are many who set off down this road, but precious few who arrive at the other end; and those who do get there may well find that the reality is a long way from the dream. But how do you ever get started in the first place? There is no shortage of guide books to help you find your way and if anything there seems to be more on the market than ever before, partly no doubt because of the Eighties redundancy rush. You have your golden handshake so what do you do – you open a pub. Perhaps the most comprehensive guide available is the text book of the Brewer's Society – *Innkeeping – a Manual for Licensed Victuallers*. I rather like that phrase "licensed victualler"; it suggests a proper seriousness of purpose. The manual is certainly not a laugh a minute, and after wading through it you might feel like entering some less demanding profession, such as neurosurgery or molecular engineering. But at least it does lay down the rules in detail, marking out the complex maze of the law through which all who keep a pub must thread their way. And one thing you must establish before you even start out is whether or not you are likely to be granted a licence – and to achieve that end both you and the premises will need a clean bill. The 1869 Wine and Beerhouse Act set out grounds for refusing a licence.

> Failure by the applicant to produce satisfactory evidence of good character.
> That the premises, or adjacent premises owned or occupied by the applicant, are of disorderly character, or frequented by thieves, prostitutes, or persons of bad character.
> That a licence previously held by the applicant has been forfeited by his misconduct, or that he has been disqualified by misconduct from receiving such a licence.

I must say I can think of several pubs which fall foul of the second rule, particularly that bit about serving bad characters. There was a time when I used to drink regularly in a pub in London, where the clientele included all three categories of undesirable patrons – not to mention such dubious characters as musicians and impoverished writers. It was an establishment which in many ways could have strayed from the pages of a Dickensian novel, not because of its outward appearance but because of the great richness and diversity of experience you could hear being discussed within its walls. It was a place where you could meet both saint and sinner, and whatever the licensing justices might say to the contrary I cannot imagine a successful pub that didn't find room for them both.

Assuming that the would-be licensee has not been spending time at Her Majesty's Pleasure or is debarred on any other grounds, then all that is needed is the pub. There are three basic ways of getting to run a pub: as a manager, as a tenant of a tied house or as a freehold owner. The manager is just what you would expect: a paid employee of the owners who manages a pub just as a shop manager looks after a shop. It is a long way from that dream of independence that glows before the eyes of the would-be licensee. It is, however, a system much in favour with many breweries. They pay a salary and get to keep the profits. In return, the manager can at least be assured of a steady, reliable income. Whether it is a good arrangement for the customer is quite a different matter: in my experience it seldom is. Too often the manager is put into a small pub, which he sees as a stepping stone on his way to better things. How is he to make the vital step? Obviously by impressing the bosses with increased profits, and one way in which we have all seen this done is by "special attractions" that can fill the place for a night. Disgruntled regulars may not like it, and may vote with their feet by moving to another pub. But it takes a time for a regular to decide to take such drastic measures, and all the while the short term profits are rising. If he goes up high enough and fast enough, the successful manager will be well on his way before decline sets in again. Novelty cannot remain novelty for long, and when the specials are over and Mexican night is no more than the stains of crusted enchilada on the carpet and the beret hung on the hook behind the bar is the last reminder of La Nuit Parisienne, what is left? A pub with no regulars who are all now comfortably settled in at the rival up the road. The brewers swear that it does not work like that, that it is a system that works to everyone's advantage. I remain sceptical.

The commonest way of getting behind the bar of your own pub is as a tenant. The tied house system, in which the brewery owns the property and then rents it out on the condition that the tenant buys his stocks from the brewers is not, as some claim, a practice hallowed by tradition. In fact, it has only existed for around one hundred years – and the story of its introduction says a good deal about just why it is so popular today, with the brewers that is. It began in the last century when brewers began to lend money to publicans in London so that they could buy pubs. The publican paid interest as he would on any other loan, but also agreed to take the brewer's beer. It was a cosy little arrangement between the London pub and the London brewer, but it was badly upset when the brewing capital of Burton came to town. Burton brewers offered a similar deal, but now they could supply the new pale ale to challenge the old porter. The customers approved, but the London brewers most definitely did not. They responded with "Burtonized" beer, which they supplied to their own regulars and, more importantly, they started to buy up pubs to protect their trade against the invaders. Now it stands to reason that the bigger you are, the more you can buy. The private breweries became public companies acquiring capital for the purchases – and a process began of big companies eating little companies thereby acquiring a whole new set of pubs for their trade. The process still goes on and is, according to the big men, a necessary process. Yet one of the biggest of all brewers, Guinness, has never had tied houses and seems to manage perfectly well without them. But our concern here is with the landlord and his customers. What does it mean to them?

Suppose you are a proud landlord of a delightful pub, tied to Bloggs Brewery, a tiny but much respected concern whose characterful beers are much appreciated by your regulars and, indeed, much appreciated by yourself. It may even have been the fame of B.B.B. – Bloggs Best Bitter – that took you there in the first place. Then the news is broken. Bloggs have fallen prey to Mighty Megafizz, the brewing branch of Supercapital International. Soon Bloggs Brewery is closed and the Megafizz tankers are appearing at the door. You don't want Megafizz, your customers don't want Megafizz, but you are going to get Megafizz, like it or not. This is a part of the way in which the system works. Some years ago I went with my family on holiday by horsedrawn caravan in Norfolk. Before we left, we were given a map covered in red warning signs. These were, I was told, Watney pubs. There were an awful lot of them, thanks to Watney's policy of buying up smaller breweries and, which was worse, closing them down together with many of the smaller village pubs they served. Not surprisingly, at that time the name Watney was about as popular as a pork sausage in a synagogue.

The tenant, however, does have an opportunity to stamp his own personality on a pub and can work in the knowledge that increased profits will benefit himself as much as the owner. There can be advantages as well as drawbacks to the system. For some, the very word "improvement" sends a shudder down the spine. How many little boozers, full of real character, have been "improved" by the addition of fake, "olde worlde" details dreamed up by an interior designer who would never be caught dead in such a place himself. On the other hand, there have been some terrible pubs where Public Bar meant bare lino, plastic tables and all the friendly charm of a casualty out-patients department. The breweries can command finance in a way that few individuals do. The move back to the single bar is a blessing for the hard pressed understaffed landlord who previously spent his time trying to be in two places simultaneously. Some had their own solutions to that problem. In my old village local, you could have died of thirst waiting to be served in the lounge, which no regular was ever known to enter.

Those who want genuine freedom can take a free house. All you need is a great deal – sometimes a very great deal – of money. You have the freedom to buy beer where you choose and, equally importantly, to buy other drinks where you like as well. For it is not only beer that is tied to most tied houses. I was recently shown a price list where the landlord was paying more for wine and spirits from the brewery than he would have paid had he bought them at the supermarket round the corner. And I had better say, to avoid any misconceptions, that it was a pub some way from my own home town. But independence comes with a price tag: freedom to do as you please also means freedom to go broke when you please. There is no security in a free house, no-one to pick up the bills when the roof blows off in a gale, no-one to help out when the factory on the corner closes down, leaving an empty room where the lunchtime crowd used to be. Yet in spite of all the evident problems, there are always plenty around who want to go into the business. They dream of the day when they can saunter down to the bar at opening time and begin to chat about matters of deep moment as the friendly, jolly customers wander in. The reality of a landlord's day is rather different.

I last worked behind pub bars in my student days, and one particular establishment was noted for its less than altogether

98

honest practices. I mentioned one such practice, briefly in a previous chapter. Inevitably, when pulling beer through a hand pump into a glass which must be filled to the brim, there will be a certain amount of spillage which collects in a tray beneath the tap. This is pure waste, or should be. Not in this pub: it joined the remnants from unfinished glasses in the barrel of mild, a dark mixture whose darkness hid a multitude of sins. All this addition of flat, stale beer might have been noticed, but the addition of a bottle of something bright and fizzy would always liven it up again. Oddly enough, we used to be complimented on its rich flavour – if only they had known just how rich it was. I know it put me off mild for years. At least there was some body in what was put back into the mild, unlike the very prevalent London practice of watering the beer at the beginning of the century. It was a practice which lasted for a very long time, and gave rise to a popular song:

> I am the man, the very fat man
> That waters the workers' beer.
> I am the man, the very fat man
> That waters the workers' beer
> And what do I care if it makes them ill
> Or turns them horribly queer:
> I've got a yacht and an aeroplane
> And I waters the workers' beer.

Practically the only good thing you can say for keg beer is that it cannot be adulterated in the same way.

Nowadays things have definitely improved, but I had rather lost touch with the art of pub-keeping, so I arranged to spend some time with Gary and Patricia Nicholson at The Beehive in Abingdon. Their day starts a good deal earlier than those with rosy dreams of peaceful days in country inns might expect. Monday to Saturday the doors are open at ten in the morning which means Gary needs to be in there around eight to start getting ready. Jobs to be done begin with bottling up – checking the shelves to see what needs replacing, then humping out the empties and hauling in the crates of replacements, which in this pub involves a lot of light ale being carried around. Light ale it may be but it is heavy work. Perhaps the most important area is the cellar, which is not necessarily under the pub – the name simply means quite literally a set of cells, a place where things can be stored. In the pub, it is the place for storing beer. The underground cellar can have advantages for it is easier to keep at an even temperature, one of the basic requirements for good draught beer. The ideal varies with different brews, but is generally between 12 and 15°C. If you are too high the active real ale will start to froth and foam; too low and it tends to go cloudy – the "warm" beer which Americans find so bewildering is simply beer kept in ideal conditions. We have now developed a palate that accepts beer at room temperature, they prefer it lower. This can lead to misunderstandings.

I walked into a bar in Canada with an English friend who asked in an impeccable British accent if the bartender would mind "taking the chill off" his beer, a remark that was greeted with total incomprehension. Elaboration followed and incomprehension was replaced by incredulity.

"You want it hot?" enquired the barman.
"Well, not exactly *hot* – just a touch warm."

Muttering to himself, the barman disappeared to return some time later with a glass containing a bubbling, steaming liquid. He slammed it down with a look that allowed no room for argument. My colleague drank this vile, boiled ale. I took my beer cold. But, to return to the English cellar – the underground cellar is not only useful but can have a romantic history. I recently visited the Ring o' Bells in Halifax, an establishment notable among other delights for its black pudding and peas. It is an eighteenth-century pub, but the cellars are part of a much older monastic building. The landlord, Stewart Reid, showed me round, but it was his wife Rozz who told the story of the ghost, a friendly rather than a malevolent creature, known to the locals as Wally. I confess to being a sceptic in such matters, and why should a ghost haunt such a cheery place unless it favoured black pudding and a pint? It was only on a second visit that I was shown the special feature of the cellar – the gravestone set into the wall. It makes you think. But that is enough of diversion, and we shall return to the much more serious matter of how to look after beer in a cellar.

The brewery may deliver a barrel of the most perfect beer imaginable, but if the landlord does not do his cellar work well, all will be in vain. My Beehive visit coincided with delivery day. There is more to this than heaving in a few crates of beer, then rolling in the barrels and fastening them into the supply system. We come back to that important fact that live beer is different from the dead keg beers, and like any other live thing it must be handled with kindness or it can turn quite nasty. What you have is a barrel of beer which is not yet ready to be drunk but is nevertheless working away quietly all the time. Two things need to happen: the sediment needs to settle and the carbon dioxide needs to be got out. Inevitably there is a whole vocabulary to learn, for the professionals will tell you that the cask has to be scotched on the stillion and spiled. In plain language, it has to be set in place and kept there by wooden wedges. Then a plug in the top of the cask has to be knocked through and replaced by a tapered wooden plug. When ready for use, the tap needs to be knocked into the front with a mallet – not tentatively, not halfheartedly, but with one clean stroke. After that, the barrel needs to be checked daily for the level of beer and then lifted if necessary by moving the wooden wedges. All of this requires skill and practice and a certain amount of hard physical effort is needed to move the 18 gallon kilderkins or kils around. And all will be wasted if the pipes connecting the barrel to the pump are not kept clean. Gary does his once a week and you can see why some less scrupulous landlords are not so keen. The pipes contain a good deal of beer which is all going to be washed away.

There are other jobs still to be done – cleaning and polishing, including the brasswork which always seems somehow to be part of the pub scene and, somewhat less romantically, the loos have to be done. And the pub is a business: account books have to be kept up to date, VAT forms have to be filled in, there is cash to bank and change to acquire. These are all jobs that have to be done in the landlord's "free time" when the pub is closed. At ten o'clock the doors are opened and stay open until 2.30 when the last pint is being pulled. But no-one ever seems desperately keen to leave on the stroke of closing time, and the legal ten minute drinking up time can be extended into chatting time as the argument on who scored the winning goal in the 1978 cup final goes into extra time. This is a typical morning, but there is some relief on Sundays when opening is from 12 to 2; but then to balance that there is Monday, market day, and an extension to 4 pm. It sometimes seems that there is scarcely time to clear up, clean down the tables, wash the glasses and empty the ash trays before 6 o'clock arrives and another five hour stint behind the bar. And even then the day does not end at closing time, for everything needs to be cleared away ready for the whole process to start again the next day. So, would-be landlord, if you fancy a seven day week with an official nine and a half hours day and numerous hours of unpaid overtime on top of that, then pubkeeping might be just the life for you. But so far, we have only looked at one side of the partnership. Gary's wife Patricia is as important as he is to the life of the pub.

Tenancies are still the backbone of the pub trade and, one hopes, will continue to dominate over managed houses. But when the brewery comes to look at prospective tenants, they are generally looking not for one person but for two. The landlady is at least as important in their eyes as the landlord. No-one can expect to run a pub single-handed, and in many small pubs the profits do not run to a large bar staff. So the wife must play her part, and not just in helping out behind the bar. Food has become increasingly important in the life of the pub and, as a general rule, where the cellar is the male preserve the kitchen usually belongs to the landlady. I do know pubs where the opposite applies, where the landlord is an enthusiastic cook and the wife pulls the pints, but they are very, very rare. Publicans do tend to be a somewhat traditional and conservative breed. But even this is still only a part of the story. The atmosphere of the pub is set as much as anything by the characters of those who run it – and that means the characters of both the parties. For all the customers know they may fight like cats and dogs after closing time, but out in front all must be sweetness and light. One of the pair may be the cheeriest, kindest soul in the world, but if the other is a grumpy slouch then all the virtues of the first might just as well not exist. No one wants to see a gloomy face across the bar. There is, in fact, a golden rule for all who work in pubs. You must listen to every customer's woes with sympathy: but never tell them yours.

What other delights can you expect in this rewarding occupation? There is always the little matter of the law to contend with, and a good many legal niceties that can spin a web around the publican. Can you refuse to serve a customer? If you are an innkeeper – and that is defined as one who has regular accommodation available as well as food and drink – then the answer is that you cannot, unless you have very good grounds indeed. As a publican, however, you can refuse anyone you like – almost. If you refuse to serve someone of a different race or colour then you had better have a very good reason for doing so or you can be prosecuted under the Race Relations Act. There is also this interesting little problem. You are in the business of selling intoxicating drinks: but if the customer actually does get legless then you too have fallen foul of the law. You should have refused to serve them. This is fine in theory, but if old Henry who has been a good customer for twenty years demands one pint too many, what are you going to do about it? Risk losing old Henry's custom or risk a run in with the law? Dilemmas like this turn up all the time over all kinds of matters. The publican who can put his hand on his heart and swear that he has never, never broken the law is either an atrocious liar or just too good for this world.

Why does anyone after all this, ever keep a pub at all? The answer must lie with the institution itself. They go into the pub for the same reason that we the customers go into it: because they enjoy its unique atmosphere, of which they will now be the guardians. They enjoy the variety of humanity that will appear across the threshold, and are the sort of people who can cope with its quirks and oddities. Thomas Burke gave his list of requirements half a century ago and he in turn looked back to an earlier age:

Centuries ago, John Earle defined the bar as the busy man's recreation, the melancholy man's sanctuary, the stranger's welcome, the scholar's kindness, and the citizen's courtesy. To keep such a place, where all men's angles may find their niche, is a task for a man of parts, a true husbandman and householder. He must, in a large way, perform the office of the ordinary family man, and must find his life's pleasure in performing it. . . . He must know something of everything, and so talk business with the commercial man, sport with the plus-fours man, crime with the morbid man, high finance with the stockbroker's clerk, and the shortcomings of the local Council with fellow-tradesmen.

Things have not changed much since then. Given such a list, I am always amazed that anyone should want to take on the job. I am eternally grateful that they do.

6. Signs of the Times

The pub sign is such a familiar part of the British street scene that it is easy to overlook or forget its significance. Often the sign is a repository of local history, sometimes it is an object of curiosity and at others a real puzzle. Take the pub we were looking at in the last chapter, The Beehive. It has, as you would expect, a sign showing a hive with bees buzzing in and out, but it is also graced by this verse:

> Within this hive we are all alive
> Good liquor makes us funny
> If you be dry step in and try
> The value of our honey.

All very nice, but why is it there in the middle of a busy market town? Could it be because the landlord in 1860 was a Mr William Honey – or was it The Beehive that attracted Mr Honey in the first place? No one seems to know, but this Beehive is by no means the only one. There is another with a similar rhyme at Penrith. But the most famous was undoubtedly The Beehive at Grantham, which took its name from an actual beehive with live bees in a tree by the door, and these lines to go with it:

> Stop traveller, this wondrous sign explore
> And say, when thou hast viewed it o'er and o'er;
> Grantham, now too rareties are thine
> A lofty steeple and a living sign.

I took a wander around the town of Abingdon, and found that The Beehive was not the only one to pose a few conundrums. Popular legend has it that The Broad Face is a macabre allusion to the swollen faces of the prisoners hanged in the old gaol across the road. Sadly, for legend, the pub name predates the building of the gaol and the mystery remains. Other pubs, however, reflect important aspects of the history of the town in their signs.

The sign painter from William Hogarth's Beer Street.

Finding a Railway Inn in Station Yard scarcely stretches the imagination in working out its origin. But the railway has now gone and the pub and its sign remain as survivors from the past – and something more, for the sign shows quite precisely just what was here. It shows the old station and, more importantly, it shows the old 7 ft broad gauge of Brunel's Great Western Railway. Other pubs and their signs reflect other aspects of the town and indeed of transport history. Any local will tell you how The Magic Midget got its name – but will the same be true a hundred years from now? Will there be fanciful stories of travelling circuses and the like, or will people remember that Abingdon was home to the makers of one of the best loved sports cars of the country, the MG, once built where the pub now stands? It may survive or it may not. Sadly, too many breweries and landlords take a pub, can make no sense of the name and change it. A little research would often have unearthed the story and then, with the addition of a little imagination, the story might even have been used to attract custom.

I used to visit a pub in the Derbyshire hills called The Light Railway. It seemed an odd name, given the pub's location, until you found that it did indeed once stand at the end of the long defunct Leek and Manifold Valley Light Railway. You can, in fact, still take a delightful walk along the track of the old line. Now the pub has changed – in some ways for the good, for it now has better beer on sale than it had in the past. But with the changes there has also been a change of name to The Manifold Valley, a link with the past has been lost. Perhaps there should be an authority that could list names for preservation just as they do buildings.

Turn to any list of pubs in any area of Britain and you will find a great deal to intrigue and baffle. There will be plenty of obvious ones: no shortage of Ploughs in agricultural areas, and plenty of Dukes this and Lords that to show who was the important man of the region. Even the latter, however, can become a bit of a puzzlement if the sign takes you a step away from the original. Strangers to the area who are not particularly well versed in heraldry might well raise an eyebrow at The Bear and Ragged

Staff at Cumnor, near Oxford, but it turns out to be no more than the emblem of the Earl of Warwick. Staying in the Oxfordshire area what can you make of the Rampant Cat or the Gate Hangs High? Is the Tite Inn a punning name or does it have special significance? Who was the Wise Alderman or his opposite number the Morris Clown? It can be quite fun hunting down the answers. Take the last two, for example. Alderman Wise was a much revered worthy of the village of Kidlington, and the pub neatly reverses surname and title; while the Morris Clown has, unlike the Magic Midget, nothing to do with the local motor industry but looks back to Bampton's long tradition of Morris dancing. How many good stories lie behind the inn signs? Well, we shall look at a few but there is a question to be answered first. Why have inn signs at all?

The story goes so far back in time that no beginning can be given to it. In an age when literacy was limited to a very few, anyone who had anything at all for sale or even just wanted to advertise their presence, had to put up a sign. The butcher, the baker and the candlestick maker all had recognizable signs, but few have survived into the present time. The barber's pole is one of the few that has lasted, its red and white stripes indicating blood and bandages – not a sign of ferociousness with the scissors but advertising the barber's other traditional function as blood letter and surgeon. The inn sign is the other great survivor. It was, in fact, the first sign to be touched on by the law. It was a statute of Richard II that singled out the brewer of ale as being the only tradesman legally forced to hang out a sign. At first all that was needed was the common sign of the trade, which was originally a simple and obvious device such as a garland of vine leaves. Later, the alehouse became recognized by a pole or brush on which an ale garland of flowers was hung when a new brew was ready for tasting. The brush is shown in medieval illustrations of alehouses. Why a brush? The brewing of beer needs yeast, which is difficult to keep. One answer was to stir a batch with a little brush. The yeast would cling to the twigs and if hung up outside could be kept well aerated. When you were ready to brew, you dunked your brush into the liquid to get fermentation under way. You could also use the brush to stir up a wine or beer that had lost its sparkle – hence the saying, "a good wine needs no brush".

Later, the alehouse came to be recognized by a red lattice window. In the days when glass was a very expensive luxury, the lattice allowed a little fresh air into the house. It had another advantage in that those within could see out, but the passer-by could not easily see in – very useful if you have stopped for a quick one and the boss is coming down the street. In 1632, the dramatist Thomas Dekker wrote that "a whole street is in some places but a continuous alehouse, not a shop to be seen between red lattice and red lattice." That presented a problem. You wanted to meet a mate for a drink, but you could hardly say "see you at the Red Lattice" if every place in the street looked the same. So in came the distinguishing sign – the pub sign that we all know today.

John Taylor, our friend the waterman poet, listed the pubs you would find on a seventeenth-century pub crawl through London. There seems to have been something of a paucity of imagination for there were 5 Angels, 4 Anchors, 6 Bells, 5 Bulls Heads, 4 Black Bulls, 4 Bears, 5 Bears and Dolphins, 10 Castles and so on ending in 33 Maidenheads. He changed the name of his own pub in Long Acre to cash in on the fame of his poetry – and also, no doubt, because Kings Head did not somehow seem the ideal name just after the execution of Charles I. Here are his own words that went with the new sign of The Poet's Head:

My signe was once a Crowne, but now it is
Changed by a sudden metamorphosis.
The crowne was taken downe, and in the stead
Is placed John Taylor's, or the Poet's Head.
A painter did my picture gratis make,
And (for a signe) I hanged it for his sake.
Now if my picture's drawing can prevayle
'Twill draw my friends to me, and I'll draw ale.

Yet even as late as the eighteenth century, signs were still being used to guide people around the streets of the town. In *A New View of London* of 1708, a wonderful new notion was described:

"In Prescott Street, Goodman's Fields, instead of signs the houses are distinguished by numbers". Even so, most people's addresses were like this one from the same period: "At her house, the Red Bull and Acorn, over against the Globe Tavern, in Queen Street, Cheapside near the Three Crowns". It sounds complex, but the pub sign remains a splendidly convenient landmark. If ever my father gave directions to anyone to go almost anywhere in the country – a thing he was often doing, for he was a much travelled man – they were always in the form of "go past the Goat and Compass, turn left at the Queen's Head and keep going until you reach the Black Bull. . .".

So, along with the new names, came the new painted signs and almost inevitably competition set in to see who could produce the grandest and finest. From being boards stuck flat onto the sides of houses, they became signs hung on brackets and eventually they were slung right across from one side of the street to the other. The most expensive ever recorded was the White Hart at Scole in Norfolk, which had twenty-five life-size figures in a hunting scene and was said to have cost a thousand pounds in 1655. Even allowing for exaggeration, this is an incredible sum of money. It is always difficult to turn costs from one period into costs for another so I have done a calculation in what seems an appropriate unit – pints of beer. And on that basis you are talking about something going on for one hundred thousand pints worth of pub sign. That is an awful lot of beer to have to sell before you get your money back. The sign alas has long gone but the White Hart remains and I can heartily recommend its public bar in particular for good beer, good fare and the atmosphere of the old country kitchen style inn with flagged floors, high settles, scrubbed tables and a roaring fire in winter. One inn that does retain its "gallows sign" as these monstrous advertisements were called, is the George at Stamford, where the sign stretches in all its grandeur right across the main street. A French writer described the signs of Charles II's reign:

> At London, they are commonly very large, and jut out so far, that in some narrow streets they touch one another; nay, and

run across almost quite to the other side. They are generally supported with carvings and gildings; and there are several that, with the branches of iron that support them, cost above a hundred guineas . . . out of London, and particularly in London, the signs of inns are suspended in the middle of a great wooden portal which may be looked upon as a kind of triumphal arch to the honour of Bacchus.

Such elaborate signs may have looked very fine, but could be decidedly dangerous. In a much publicized accident in 1718 a Fleet Street sign collapsed bringing the wall down with it and killing two passers-by. The days of the huge sign were over.

Any large town should be able to boast a rich variety of signs, each of which will have its own story to tell. A very entertaining book *In Praise of Ale* written by W. T. Marchant in 1888 has this poem called "Signs of Love at Oxford":

She's as light as the *Greyhound*, and fair as the *Angel*,
Her looks than the *Mitre* more sanctified are;
But she flies like the *Roebuck*, and leaves me to rage ill,
Still looking to her as my true Polar *Star*.

New Inn-ventions I try, with new art to adore,
But my fate is, alas! to be voted a *Boar;*
My *Goats* I forsook to contemplate her charms,
And must own she is fit for our noble *King's Arms*.

Now *Cross*'d and now *Jockey*'d, now sad, now elate,
The *Chequers* appear but a map of my fate;
I blush'd like a *Blue*-cur to send her a *Pheasant*,
But she called me a *Turk*, and rejected my present.

So I moped to the *Barley Mow*, griev'd in my mind,
That the *Ark* from the flood ever rescued mankind!
In my dreams *Lions* roar, and the *Green Dragon* grins;
And fiends rise in the shape of the *Seven Deadly Sins*.

111

When I ogle the *Bells*, should I see her approach,
I skip like a *Nag* and jump into a *Coach;*
She is crimson and white like a *Shoulder of Mutton*,
Not the red of the *Ox* was so bright when first put on;

Like the *Hollybush* prickles she scratches my liver.
While I moan and I die like the *Swan* by the river.

Oxford can boast a good few pubs not on the list – and one or two
that are there have since disappeared or changed their names. I am
sorry the Seven Deadly Sins is no longer with us: we have four
Seven Stars in the area, and a touch of sin would make a welcome
change. Poems about pubs are few, but John Taylor is by no
means the only landlord to have a poem as part of his sign. In
general such poems were humorous like this one at the Mortal
Man in Troutbeck:

O mortal man, that lives by bread,
What is it makes thy nose so red?
Thou silly fool that looks so pale
'Tis drinking Sally Birkett's Ale.

The same humour that advertised the pub in life, was occasionally
used as advertising, even when he was in his grave. This epitaph is
from Upton-on-Severn:

Beneath this stone in hope of Zion
Doth lie the landlord of "The Lion":
Resigned unto the heavenly will,
His son keeps on the business still

which one might describe as the gravestone as inn sign. My
favourite boozy epitaph is this, even if it doesn't double as an
advert for the pub up the road:

Poor John Scott lies buried here;
Tho' once he was both *hale* and *stout*,

112

Death stretched him on his *bitter bier;*
In another world he *hops* about.

Words, however, are of comparatively minor importance: what really matters on a pub sign is the picture that catches the eye. Occasionally the famous turned their hands to the inn sign – artists as varied in style as Millais and Mervyn Peake, and you cannot get a much greater contrast than that. One famous artist is himself portrayed on many a pub in Oxfordshire and Berkshire. George Morland, the eighteenth-century painter, did do the occasional sign, but he is now seen because Morland the brewers use him as their own trademark, pictured with a palate in one hand and a glass in the other. But it is rare to find the famous indulging in such practices – and given the level of payment by most breweries, this is not too surprising. It is in any case a somewhat specialist job, requiring special skills and techniques, so I went along to see a painter who, with 322 signs to his credit, should know something about the craft.

Darrell Gardner trained as a horticulturist, but found an even greater satisfaction in painting flowers than in growing them. Today, he is an artist with an established and growing reputation – but at the beginning of his career he needed something regular to pay the bills. I am not sure if it was being born with the name Gardner that took him into gardening, but I can hazard a pretty good guess as to what turned his attention towards the pub sign. This, however, is not a job you can take on straight away, whatever talents you may possess. There is a trade to be learned, and Darrell learned the old fashioned way as assistant to a sign writer who had, in turn, learned his trade in the world of circus. Darrell soon discovered that good lettering was as important a part of the sign as good painting. He also learned the great lesson that a successful sign, whether for pub or circus, has to satisfy several criteria: it must be bright enough and clear enough to be seen from a distance and to make its point from a distance; and it should never stray too far from established tradition. Above everything else, the sign must please the pub customers – they are the final arbiters, critics and judges. For if they don't like it, the

113

brewery will take it down without waiting for a second opinion. You also need to be wary of the expert lurking in the background but ever ready to pounce. Darrell was once asked to do a sign for The Imperial in Tunbridge Wells. All over the place you can find King's Heads and Queen's Heads and all kinds of royal pates, so for a change he turned to the world of nature and painted the big and beautiful Monarch butterfly. And that's where he fell foul of the expert, who objected on the grounds that it was not the Imperial. But the actual Imperial lives in South America, whilst the Monarch is a visitor – if an infrequent one – to these shores. And the Monarch is beautiful, so the sign stayed, in defiance of the pedants. But I have to say that he passed my test with flying colours, even if the flying colours of the butterfly failed to please everyone. Looking through Darrell's photograph album, I came across two signs which I had already seen and specially noted for their accuracy. One was in Faversham, and showed a windmill; the other was in Tenterden and had paintings of a pair of locomotives which still run on the nearby Kent and East Sussex Railway: a good old British centenarian on one side and one of the company's American engines on the other. I could find no technical faults with either. A lot of care and research had obviously gone into them. So how does a new sign develop from a note in the brewer's desk diary to a colourful board swaying in the wind?

The process is initiated by the brewery surveyor, who decides when a new sign is required. How much care is then given to the selection of a suitable board depends very much on the individual brewery. Matters will of course be quite different for a free house, where the owner will often have very strong personal preferences. In the case of Shepherd Neame, however, for whom Darrell has done much of his work, the high quality of the signs reflects the personal enthusiasm of Basil Neame. So, the surveyor approaches the artist, often with little more than the name of the house and no fixed idea of what form the sign should take. Darrell was asked to do the Admiral's Walk in Sheerness and as it was a fine old inn, he felt that it deserved a sign with real historical character. The image he had in mind was of Nelson walking along a quay that was just as it would have been in his day. That meant considerable research into illustrations of the docks in the early nineteenth century and a trip to the National Maritime Museum to study portraits of Nelson. At this stage there was still no guarantee that the design would be accepted, and he had to complete a 10 by 6 inch water-colour to put up for approval. And here one must remember that you can produce the most paintily masterpiece of the age and it still might not work as a pub sign. The artist also has to think of self interest in this and remember that, if he gets the job, he has to produce the final painting not once but twice – once for each side of the board, and the two signs must be identical. The more complex the picture, the harder it will be to copy.

Assuming the design is accepted, work can start and he will have to use tools and materials appropriate to the job in hand. Special sign painter's brushes are needed and, inevitably, they are costly items. The actual paints have to be carefully chosen. House paints and ordinary enamels can be used on inn signs, but when you want those intense colours that make the whole picture sing out and call the passers-by's attention, then you have to go for special paints. Here again you come across tradition, for Keeps of London have been meeting just that need of sign painters with a range called Intenso, and they have been doing so for the best part of two hundred years. Like the sign painter's brushes, they do not come cheap either. But that expense pales when set against a board that calls for gold. Remember, the board will hang out in all seasons and all weathers and is expected to last for at least six years. Ordinary gold paint is no use here, for it would soon tarnish and dull: gold leaf is the only answer. So Darrell has had to learn the craft of the gilder as well as that of the sign painter.

Sign painting needs to be bold and needs to be done at speed: the comparatively low fees paid to sign painters work as an added encouragement to rapidity. A side a day is the ideal to aim for, but here again special techniques need to be employed. These are very different from those of the easel painter hoping to make it to the Royal Academy. The techniques impose their own limitations, for colours need to be layered, one on top of the other. You have to wait for each layer to dry before the next goes on – but equally you have to have the experience to know just which colours can be layered on to others, for not every combination can be made to work. Individual signs can present their own special problems, especially those involving coats of arms and heraldic devices. The design has to go to the Herald's Office for designs and colours to be checked and that original design must be reproduced with absolute fidelity – no approximations are allowed here. Everything has to be just so or down must come the sign. So, suppose you have a quite common pub name such as the Royal Standard. It is a Georgian pub, so the shield of the House of Hanover might seem appropriate: a decision the painter might later regret, for it is a complex affair. The emblem is a quartered shield with different devices in each corner. They all have proper heraldic names but, in lay terms, you have a mixture of lions, fleur de lys, a harp and a horse. First you paint one quarter on one side, then you take a tracing and carry that over to the reverse. Then you add the second quarter, trace and carry over – and so the design goes backwards and forwards from one side to the other until all is complete. You should end up with two sides that are heraldically accurate and a perfect match. After that you thank heaven that your next job is the Three Horseshoes!

Darrell has had his share of problems in his time. Some heraldic signs can present special difficulties in research, such as the Divers' Arms, for deep sea divers do indeed have their very own official coat of arms. Mostly the problems can be solved without too much difficulty, but there is one that has been troubling him for years. The Bonny Cravat is another pub in the Tenterden area, but where on earth does the name originate? One theory has it that it relates to a uniform worn by Cromwell's troops, though that seems a touch dubious. A second has it that a French prisoner of war in Napoleonic times was well treated by mine host of the day and gave the landlord a tie and tiepin as a thank-you. It sounds a touch more reasonable. His latest discovery is that there was once a game called Cravat and I can add my own macabre twopennyworth with the information that Cravat was once also a euphemism for the hangman's noose. Which is the true origin?

No-one seems to know and until the answer is found the true sign will remain unpainted.

One of the problems lies in the way in which pub names get distorted over the years. Sometimes it is just a bit of local fun. Pubs can get a bit above themselves with all this College of Heralds stuff, so the locals turn the Swan and Harp into the Goose and Gridiron. In other cases, we simply forget our history. The old Saxon practice of marking the drinking bowl with pegs and drinking a wassail of good health disappeared so far back into history that no-one any longer remembers why the village inn was the Peg and Wassail and the Pig and Whistle was born. These are the sort of problems that ensure that the life of the pub sign artist is never a dull one.

Every pub name has a story. The Drover's Arms high on the moors brings memories of the days when cattle were brought to market on the hoof and flocks of geese would be driven a hundred miles and more to be sold at the Christmas markets. Famous men are recorded on inn signs, even if no-one is any longer certain who they were or why they were famous. My home area of Yorkshire was positively littered with Marquises of Granby but I never had the faintest idea of who he was. Robert Graves put his doubts into these verses on the General Elliott at Ferry Hinksey:

The postman cannot well recall,
The ostler never knew
Whether that day was Malplaquet
The Boyne or Waterloo.

And paint shall keep his buttons bright
Though all the world's forgot
Whether he died for England's pride
By bottle or by pot.

In fact, he was in charge of the garrison at Gibraltar, which he commanded and defended against the Spanish. And you can find him again, still battling on, in Leeds as well.

So many pubs, so many signs and so many stories – and so little space to tell them; so here by way of a sample is a lexicon of locals or alehouse alphabet.

Axe and Compass: this is a good one to start with, for it stands for a whole range of signs belonging to particular trades and professions. It represents the arms of the Company of Carpenters, and you can find it all over Britain.

Bladud Arms, Bath: Now I have to confess that I don't know this pub but the description in *The Good Beer Guide*, the drinking man's Bible, is so wonderfully terse and enigmatic that it had to go in. "Named after a local swineherd and prince who cured himself and his pigs of leprosy." What else can one say!

Champion of the Thames: A Cambridge pub with a name to send all Oxford men reaching for their oars, probably to use as cudgels.

The Drunken Duck, Barngates: According to the story, a landlady went out one day and found all her ducks inexplicably dead. Saddened but unwilling to waste a good duck she began to pluck the moribund quackers. She almost had the last of them down to their skins when they all began to wake up, not dead it seems but dead drunk having sipped at a leaking barrel. The mortified landlady viewed the naked fowl and took compassion on them: she knitted them little waistcoats to keep out the cold. Some people will tell you that the name is all to do with one of those barbaric sports in which dogs chase ducks but I prefer the other version. It deserves to be true.

Elephant and Castle: One of the best known pub signs of them all – and again there is no shortage of explanations. Is it a corruption of Infanta da Castile? Or is it the crest of the cutlers, the elephant with its howdah? You pays your money. . .

The Flying Monk, Malmesbury: A good sign and a good story from the nearby abbey, where in the eleventh century a young monk attempted to invent hang gliding with home-made wings – and failed.

The Grand Junction, Buckingham: A name instantly recognized by canal buffs as the waterway that joined London to Birmingham. But it also had numerous branches, not all of which survive, except here in a pub name.

The Hopbine Inn, Petteridge: How disappointing it would be if Kent did not have pubs which recorded the county's great contribution to the world of beer. This little pub must stand for all.

The Ivanhoe, Sprotborough: Not a name you necessarily expect to find in South Yorkshire, but a reminder that Sir Walter Scott did not do all his writing in Scotland, for a good deal of *Ivanhoe* was written in a room overlooking the River Don.

Jolly . . .: Add whatever you like afterwards, though for some reason sailors seem to predominate, but you can take your pick of the rest from anglers to waggoners. It is not surprising it is so popular: after all if you cannot be jolly in a pub where can you go? No one so far as I know has done one for marines which might be called the Jolly Jolly.

Ketton Ox, Yarm: No surprise to find that it commemorates a notably huge beast that weighed in at nearly two tons in 1806. It was a handsome beast and this is a remarkably handsome inn. Those who cherish useless information might also care to know that the nearby railway viaduct contains seven million bricks.

Live and Let Live, Downham Market: Words that should hang in every bar. The sign shows an amicable cat and dog.

The Machine Man, Long Wittenham: Not a sign that you might expect to find in the rural Thames Valley, but one which reminds us that machinery was once a true novelty down on the farm.

The North Star, Steventon: One of those common names, but here not quite what you might expect. This is no reference to astronomy but to the nearby Great Western Railway and one of its most famous steam locomotives.

Old Dungeon Ghyll, Great Langdale: For once the old is justified and distinguishes it from the New Dungeon Ghyll. Both take their name from the grand waterfalls in the nearby ravine. But the real reason for its inclusion is that this was the favourite pub of my youth, and the years have not dimmed the pleasure of calling in for a pint there.

Pack o' Cards, Combe Martin: Four floors, one for each suit, fifty-two windows. Why the card motif? Its builder made a

119

fortune at the gaming tables, and this was his monument to the luck of the cards.

Quiet Woman: Once a very common name, though not one to appeal to feminists, for the quiet woman herself was always depicted either dead or headless.

Royal Standard of England, Forty Green: There are two reasons for its inclusion. Firstly, it was one of many to claim the title "oldest pub". More interestingly perhaps it was originally The Ship, and still boasts ships timbers and furnishings. But why the nautical associations for a Buckinghamshire pub, which must be about as far as you can get from the sea? Real ale and real history meet in happy combination here.

Swan With Two Necks: Another widespread name that comes from a loss of original meaning. The Vintners Company was one of those which had the right to keep swans on the Thames, which were marked at the swan upping by two nicks on the beak. Two nicks became two necks.

Three Pilchards, Polperro: A voice from the past this, a reminder of the time when the Cornish ports were home to a vast fleet of boats which fished for pilchards. They were too successful and the pilchard vanished.

Union: A very popular name that appeared with the Act of Union that joined the kingdoms of England and Scotland. One might reasonably expect to find any pub with such a name to boast both excellent English beer and first-rate Scottish whisky. Names, alas, can be misleading.

Vulcan Inn, Newton-le-Willows: A mighty name from the past, but this Vulcan was not the God of Fire and Metal but his earthly counterpart. The local Vulcan Foundry was a great engineering works and manufacturer of steam locomotives.

Windbound, Sheppardine, Avon: A lovely name for a pub by the estuary of the Severn. Incidentally, can there be a greater bureaucratic absurdity than that places on the Severn should now appear in a county called Avon? But I can think of worse places to wait for a wind than this, and with a whole array of hand pumps and barrels to draw on, I should be in no hurry to whistle up a breeze.

XL, Garstang: It is really the Excel, but that's the way they have it on the sign.

Ye Olde . . .: Words that usually appear before the name of a perfectly decent, honest old pub that has been taken apart so that the old genuine bits can be replaced by plastic imitations.

Zoo: A whole zoo-ful of animals is available in pub names from Antelope, which is fairly common to Zebra, a much rarer beast though one is to be found in Cambridge; and here the list must end. But somehow it is difficult to say goodbye to the story of the signs, so let us end in verse, part of a poem by the Rev. John Gray, a man in love with the names of inns:

> The Plum Pudding; Wheel;
> The Merry Mouth; The Duck; The Fleece;
> The Apple, Oak, and Cocoa Trees;
> The Hatchet Inn, the Compasses;
> And Bells by Rings, and Eights, and Threes,
> The Bluebell, the Bell
>
> And so on and so;
> But in the empire of the blest,
> Where inns are old and gala-dressed.
> Their signs are not among the least
> Of good things to know.

A shove halfpenny player by Robert Wykes.

7. The Lure of Skittles

He's up to those grand games, but one of these days
I'll lure him on to skittles – and astonish him.

Henry J. Byron

Pub entertainment in our family began, in fact, with the pub signs
which formed the basis of car-borne cricket. The "batting" side
scored one run for every leg on a sign. So you got two runs for the
Green Man. There are occasional bursts of scoring that could
make Botham look like a stone-waller. In Gloucestershire I came
across a Coach and Horses with four horses, six passengers and a
driver – a grand total of forty-six in one shot. But even that was as
nothing compared with the Fox and Hounds which showed one
fox, twenty hounds, six horses and six riders, a massive match
winning 120. But a sign with no legs, such as The Trout or The
Rising Sun, meant a lost wicket. It kept the children amused for
hours, but proved a great irritation to father who was kept
constantly reminded that we were driving past pubs instead of
stopping at them.

Signs are advertisements which may be humorous but which
generally are not. Signs in pubs are often intended to amuse the
customer whilst getting a simple message across. We all know
"I've got an arrangement with my bank manager: he doesn't sell
beer and I don't cash cheques", "would customers please remain
seated while the bar is in motion" and so on. Now I always
thought these were a modern invention, probably because they
have become unusually conspicuous in the last ten years or so.
They were in fact already commonplace in the last century. Here
are a couple of nineteenth-century "don't ask me for credit"
notices. First,

MORE	BEER	SCORE	CLERK
FOR	MY	MY	THEIR
DO	TRUST	PAY	SENT
I	I	MUST	HAVE
SHALL	IF	I	BREWERS
WHAT	AND	AND	MY

which I shall leave you to work out for yourselves. Then this poem from Pateley Bridge:

The maltster doth crave
His money to have
The exciseman says have I must.
By that you can see
How the case stands with me;
So I pray you don't ask me for trust.

Then there were the practical joke signs such as this:

WYBMABIITY

The innocent customer is expected to ask what it stands for.

"Will you buy me a beer if I tell you?"

The customer is then expected to buy the beer and then demand to be told the answer.

"But I just told you" says the practical joker.

Eventually the innocent gets the message and either laughs heartily or brains his tormentor. I must confess I am not much amused by these notices, particularly when the mass produced ones have been seen a hundred times before. I don't think I would be much more amused by all the jolly japes that were once so popular. There used to be things like frog mugs, where you would drink down your beer only to reveal a frog staring up at you from

124

the bottom of the mug. But all the frog mugs I have ever seen looked totally unconvincing. Puzzle mugs were a puzzle simply because it was difficult to work out how you could drink from them without pouring beer all over your trousers – very mirth-provoking! Happily such tricks are now rare, but the pub game is still alive and well.

Games and pubs have gone together for at least as long as records exist. The Roman chequer board has already been mentioned, and there are a whole variety of games which can be seen portrayed in medieval manuscripts and which are still with us today. There are games played inside pubs and games played outside pubs; there are familiar games and esoteric games and there are some games which have now quite disappeared from view. The latter are, I suppose, of strictly historical interest but I came across one, described in Joseph Strutt's classic *The Sports and Pastimes of the People of England* (1801) which is so splendidly unlikely that I cannot resist mentioning it. It was part of the lamb-ale festival in the village of Kirtlington near Oxford. The village maidens had their thumbs tied behind their backs and were then sent out to chase and capture a fat lamb which they had to hold in their teeth. I know it all sounds incredible, but Mr Strutt is a most reliable guide in these matters and I believe him – and it seems, in fact, to have lasted into this century. The next part at least is very credible. The lamb once caught was killed and roasted and everyone sat around drinking beer. All the best pub games end with everyone sat around drinking beer. The Kirtlington booze-up, however, might be thought a little excessive as it lasted for a whole week.

Where do you begin with such a topic as pub games? Any game will do, but let us start gently and work our way up towards the more energetic pastimes. The playing of cards is one of those activities which, taken together with the pub has, in the popular imagination, always been associated with gambling. It has therefore tended to be frowned on, at the very least, by authority. There is no earthly reason why card games should not be played just for fun, but most of the more popular gambling games, such as poker and pontoon are quite simply no fun unless money changes hands. The one card game which is both widespread and popular and which can be played just for pleasure is crib or cribbage. When the seventeenth-century poet, Sir John Suckling, wrote the lines

Why so pale and wan, fond lover?
Prithee why so pale?

he had probably been trying to teach the game to his girl friend, for while it is not an excessively difficult game to play it is quite extraordinarily difficult to describe. Sir John should have managed it, however, for he was the inventor of crib. In essentials, it is a game in which the players try to combine cards to make runs, flushes, pairs and combinations that will add up to fifteen. Generally, you hold four cards in your hand and there is a card cut from the pack which is common to all players. The point is that all combinations count. So that if, for example, you are lucky enough to be holding J, Q, K, 5 and another queen was cut, you would count two points for each combination of fifteen, two for each pair and count the run according to the number in it. So in this case, each court card counting as ten, you have 4 ways of making fifteen – 8 points; one pair – two points; and two runs of 3 each making another 6 points – 16 points in all. You might also have one for his nob, but we won't go into that. That just represents a part of the game: as I said it almost defies description. If you are embarrassed at not knowing how to play and you don't wish to spoil your reputation as a good pub gamesman, then here is a phrase to get you out of a suggestion of a game with dignity: "I don't think I will thanks, I've had nothing but nineteens lately." You have established expert knowledge, for nineteen is the one score you can never make with any combination of cards at crib. In effect you have been saying that you have had a run of bad luck. It is one of those games that you hate or love, and I must confess myself an addict, and fortunate enough to live in a crib playing area with a well established league.

Even more popular is dominoes, a game which is said to originate in China, a view which seems to rest almost entirely on the similarity between Mah-jong tiles and domino bones, even though the method of play is totally different. As far as Britain is concerned, however, it has nothing to do with China, nor is it particularly old, in fact, it seems to have arrived here around the beginning of the last century having made its way over from Italy. It scarcely requires an explanation as to how it works, but it is worth considering why it works. Those who have never played, think it is just a question of someone laying down a domino or bone and if you can make the numbers match then on you go. In fact, rather like crib, it is a game where the skill lies in assessing odds and making fine calculations. There are those who claim that this is nonsense and that it is all a matter of luck. To them I would say this: go down to a pub with a well established domino school and challenge the oldest and most experienced player to a match for a pint. Continue the process until either you are broke or he is too drunk to continue – and then try and work out that it was just bad luck that made you the loser.

Another more or less sedentary game, but one which requires much skill, is shove halfpenny. It is a very simple game to describe but a good deal less easy to play well. A board is marked out by parallel lines a little more than a halfpenny diameter apart. The object is to hit the halfpenny up the board so that it falls into one of the spaces. There are nine spaces and you have five halfpennies per go, and the first player to score three halfpennies in each of the spaces wins. That could scarcely be simpler as an idea but there is a most satisfying complexity to the play, for you can use the coins on the board during your turn, bouncing off coins to get into a space or nudging one further up the board. It also has what all the best games have – ample room for argument and dispute. Is a coin clear or is it touching? Some boring boards have metal strips set into the dividing marks which can be raised and lowered. The question of whether the coin is in or not is immediately settled by seeing whether it is moved by the strip. There are local variations, including the Dorset version played on the numbered Swanage board.

The pub game par excellence is darts. Even those who have never been near a pub now know all about it from television –

though I find it one of the most tedious spectator sports in existence. This view may be touched by envy for no-one, alas, has ever had to issue that famous cry of "one hundred and eighty" when I have been playing. In the standard game you throw three darts at a board marked in segments numbered one to twenty with an outer ring that counts double, an inner ring that counts treble and two bullseyes, the middle worth fifty, the outer twenty-five. The winner is the first to reach 501, with a stipulation that the final dart must be in the double. The main requirements for darts are a steady hand, a keen eye, the ability to count backwards from 501 and, if international competitions are anything to go by, a taste for pints of lager. I have always claimed that my inability to make the pub darts team stems from my failure to meet the last requirement.

Television has not really been very good for pub darts. People seem embarrassed at not being able endlessly to hammer away at the treble twenty. One result has been a shift to other darts games such as Killer and Burma Road and the most infuriating of all, Overs and Unders. The latter is dead simple and any number can play. The first player throws three darts with the left hand, and all each individual player is required to do is beat the score of the previous thrower. Failure to do so results in loss of a life. The snag comes when you reverse the process – and need to score less. You probably think of yourself as someone like me, incapable of notching up a really big score, but just wait until you need to score three ones. You'll be whacking the arrows into the treble twenty with the regularity of an Eric Bristow. I like these odd games best, because they add to the general merriment by pulling in anyone in the pub who fancies a game. They breed good fellowship and good humour, which is what games are supposed to do but rarely seem to manage. You can go on writing about darts and its variations for pages. The origins of the game are obscure, so you can theorize to your heart's content. It does, however, seem to be generally agreed that it was a game developed for archers who preferred to be indoors with a pint rather than outdoors with a bow and arrow and no free hand to hold a jar. Local variations in boards of different sizes and different arrangements of numbers are legion, but they are steadily diminishing as the standard board of the professionals becomes ever more dominant.

These are the principal but by no means the only indoor games. In the 1890s a billiard table manufacturer, sniffing for a profit, promoted the Licenced Victuallers Billiards Tournament. It proved remarkably popular, but of course you could only enter if you had a billiard table – and the promoter of the competition, Thurston's, was only too happy to sell you one. The problem was that billiards required a great deal of space which the publicans soon realized could be better occupied by paying topers. The billiards saloons began to disappear, usually converted into bars. A particularly fine example is to be seen in the very sumptuous Railway Hotel at York – which now seems to have arisen above its mundane origins to emerge as the Royal York. The old billiards saloon was down in the basement and very lush it was too, with bright tiled walls and ornate fittings. Now it is a bar that announces itself as being devoted to the needs of railway maniacs – who it must be supposed are not also beer maniacs, for on my last visit I found that while there was real ale in the ordinary bar none had percolated down to the depths. The alternative to the full size billiards and snooker table is the bar billiards table. The skills are the same – hitting balls with a cue to try and knock them into holes, but here the players stay at one end of the table, a bit like a bagatelle board, and aim at numbered holes. Hazards are provided in the shape of wooden mushrooms: knock down a white one and you lose the break, demolish the dreaded black and your entire score is wiped out.

Bar billiards is becoming increasingly difficult to find for it has largely been replaced by pool. I find this difficult to understand. At pool, the players need to march all round the table and play shots from all angles. Inevitably far more space is required for two players to have a game than it is for bar billiards. Often, in fact, there is not enough room and players engage in weird contortions that would do credit to a yogi in order to play their shots. At least, if Shakespeare is to be believed, billiards is by far the older game for even Cleopatra was fond of the pastime. But if you really want

129

to search the annals of antiquity for a pub game, then skittles not billiards is the thing.

It was C. S. Calverley, he who hymned the praise of beer who first wrote of some happy-go-lucky characters that "Life is with such all beer and skittles", but the sport goes back a long way before his time and is first heard of as a children's game around 5000 BC. No doubt it has changed a little over the years – it must have done for there are a huge number of variations played – but the essentials remain the same: set up some pins and then try to knock them down. In my region of Oxfordshire you can find two extreme versions. One is the common skittle alley, where nine wooden pins are put up at one end and a wooden ball is rolled along the ground in an attempt to knock them down. The second is Aunt Sally, in which there is only one target, the dolly, which is a wooden peg set in a hoop at the top of an iron pole. Here the missiles are wooden batons and they take a bit of getting used to. In between are endless variations.

I am particularly fond of the Midlands variation known as Hood Skittles, which I first encountered on a very jolly evening in a fine canalside pub, the Boat at Newbold-on-Avon. This is an indoors version where the missile is neither a ball nor a baton but a "cheese", a thick wooden disc like an obese discus. There is a London version in which everything is on a grand scale with skittles over a foot high and vast cheeses weighing around ten pounds each. Even this cannot compete with a version played in the Basque country of Spain. I spent an entertaining afternoon supping wine and watching two local teams compete on a hot, cloudless day that called for frequent refreshment of the combatants. It was played in an enclosed area roughly the length of a cricket pitch. Conventional wooden pins were set in the centre but the massive balls were hurled high in the air to bombard the target. It was very spectacular, if a trifle alarming. At the opposite end of the scale, is a game which is very popular in Derbyshire and Staffordshire called Devil Among the Tailors – origin obscure as the dictionary notes. This is a table top version, where the ball is suspended from a pole and swung round in an arc to cause havoc among the pins; or not, as the case may be. This is by no means an

exhaustive list of the variations in this excellent game.
There are numerous close relations which involve throwing
things at other things: quoits where you throw hoops, ringing the
bull where you attempt to get a ring, suspended as in the Devil
Among the Tailors, on to a hook on the wall, or, more properly
on to a bull's horn, and, of course, bowls. The connection
between bowls and the pub has rather diminished over the years,
though it lives on in numerous Bowling Green pub names. In
recent years another version has come across from France,
pétanque. Here the balls are metal and not wood and are thrown
out of the back of the hand rather than rolled. Otherwise it works
on much the same idea of getting your bowl or boule close to the
jack. Pétanque has the great advantage, however, that it needs no
specially prepared surface, and a gravel path is ideal. I have not yet
quite got used to playing it when the air is heavy with the smell of
hops and barley rather than the aniseed ball aroma of Pernod.

Other outdoor games can require slightly more elaborate
equipment. There are two closely related games which, though
rare, are happily far from dead – a northern version, knurr and
spell, and a southern, bat and trap. Both rely on a mechanism to
throw a ball in the air for the player to hit. In knurr and spell a
spring set in a wooden frame, the spell, sends the ball, the knurr,
up into the air. The object is then simply to hit the knurr as far as
you can using a thing like an overgrown golf club. Bat and trap is
much the same, except that here the bat is like a big table tennis bat
and the batsman has to try and hit towards a goal whilst
contending with the efforts of a fielding side to get him out. They
can do this by catching him out or throwing the ball back so that it
hits the trap. You could think of the first as a pub version of golf
and the other as pub cricket.

That brings us rather neatly to the other aspect of the pub and
games, for the local has long had a close association with sport and
closest association of all is that between the pub and cricket. In
part, this is a happy accident in that village cricket is so often
played on the green under the gaze of the locals around the pub.
There is nothing in the world more redolent of a special sort of
English romanticism touched by humour than the game of cricket

played outside the pub door. That atmosphere has never been caught more precisely than in *England, Their England,* that most English of books, which was written by a Scotsman born in India, A. G. Macdonell. You should read the whole thing but here is a sample:

> It so happened that, at the end at which he was to bowl, the ground behind the wicket was level for a few yards and then sloped down rather abruptly, so that it was only during the last three or four intensive, galvanic yards of his run that the blacksmith, who took a long run, was visible to the batsman or indeed to anyone on the field of play except the man stationed in the deep field behind him . . . The first ball that he delivered was a high, full-pitch to leg, of appalling velocity. It must have lighted upon a bare patch among the long grass near long leg, for it rocketed, first bounce, into the hedge and four byes were reluctantly signalled by the village umpire. The row of gaffers on the rustic bench shook their heads, agreed that it was many years since four byes had been signalled on that ground, and called for more pints of old-and-mild. The other members of Mr Hodge's team blanched visibly and called for more pints of bitter. The youngish professor of ballistics, who was in next, muttered something about muzzle velocities and started to do a sum on the back of an envelope.

In their time, pubs have been host to a whole range of different sporting activities. Prize fighting was very much a pub affair, even when it was illegal. There are memories of the old bare knuckle days in the George at Odiham. Tom Sayers fought many battles there including his last contest with the American John Heenan, an event recorded in verse at the pub:

> My last fight was with Heenan who from American came
> I never fought a better man nor one who showed more game.
> For two long hours and better each tried his best to win
> And none could tell which man was beat when the ring was
>   broken in.

Not everyone approved of games and sports and there was a time when they were regarded as, if anything, even worse than the demon drink itself. That, of course, was in the days when games meant gaming and gaming meant the road to ruin and despair. This is not really true today. The pub it is true is still the place where certainties for the 2.30 at Redcar are given out with that special air of total confidence that only belongs with those who have just backed eight losers in a row. This tip, they assure you, is different – and they believe it. But the ancient pub pastime of passing illegal betting slips disappeared when the betting shops opened, and the role of the pub in the world of the gambler was at once diminished. Today, pub games may be played for small stakes – the next round being a traditional bet and one which greatly pleases the landlord – but gambling does not really account for games' continuing popularity. They survive because they promote sociability. Strangers can still walk into pubs and offer to "take the chalks" to score at darts, and so work their way into the life of the place. But a new generation has brought a different element into play. The electronic games are solitary affairs. A casual visitor drops into the pub, buys his drink and then stands staring into the whirring lights of the machine. It is not old fogeyism to deplore these newcomers, for they strike to the heart of the unique pub atmosphere. Add to that their infernal, relentless noise and you have a genuine menace. I think you could have an ideal pub with no electricity supply at all, for many of my pet hates would disappear the moment the power went off: no video games, no fruit machines, no television in the corner (the ultimate horror), nothing in fact in the way of entertainment except that which the customers could make for themselves.

Many years ago in those far off days when people crossed the Atlantic by sea rather than by air, I went to Liverpool to meet a friend from Canada who was making her first visit to Britain. She had seen pubs in films and was eager now to experience the real thing, so we went to a suitably Victorian looking establishment near the docks. I warned her that it would not be quite like the movies, but I needn't have bothered – it was more like the popular film image than I could ever have believed possible. All the trappings were there, but what made the visit truly memorable was a group of wonderful local ladies out on a celebration. Flushed they may have been, though it was certainly not with the first flush of youth, but their liveliness and verve made us the young visitors seem to be the staid and stolid ones. The grand climax came when they climbed on to the tables and did a genuine knees-up, warmly bloomered legs kicking up to the ceiling. The young lady from Canada was enchanted: this, she said, was exactly what she had expected. I hadn't the heart to tell her that in all my pub-going experience I had never seen anything quite like this and doubted if I would see it again.

The impromptu sing-song, even the occasional knees-up are an accepted part of pub life – or would be but for the weird licensing laws which determine just how much singing, dancing and general merriment is acceptable to authority. Miles' invaluable guide to licensed victuallers sums up the present position thus:

> The areas in which statutory regulation for music and dancing apply may conveniently be divided into two classes, those in which the matter is governed by a special Act of Parliament of local application, and those in which the general statutory provision mentioned later has been adopted by the local authority.

Fine! Thomas Burke knew exactly how sensible he thought the complex rules were in the 1930s.

> Though you may not sing *in* the tavern you may sing just outside it. You may carry your banjo along to the tavern, and then you may thrust your foot inside the door, and through the crevice you may bawl or croon as many songs as you know; and then you may go round the bar with your offertory bag. The law makes no objection to that – which is work. It only objects to your being cheerful in the bar without filling up a form announcing that on a given date you are going to be cheerful.

Things are not quite that bad really, for the law allows a maximum of two "live" performers to entertain without a licence. It is not clear what dire penalties will be enacted should a third join in. Best not to enquire too closely. But the impromptu sing-song round the old joanna still provides some of the most memorable and enjoyable of pub evenings – and sometimes the most surprising. I was having a pint in my local when a young man came in who I had not met before but who the landlord clearly knew well for he was at once invited to give the company a tune. He obligingly sat down and began first to play and then to sing. Now that is not perhaps too surprising, but when were you last in an ordinary little town boozer and found yourself entertained by a counter tenor? And he sang everything counter tenor from Nelly Dean to Purcell's Come All Ye Sons of Art. And the customers loved it. You can't plan things like that. You can't put up a notice saying "Sunday lunchtime – Purcell recital" not unless you fancy a pub with no customers. But this impromptu, unrehearsed and totally unexpected concert was an absolute wow.

The singalong has been with us for as long as pubs have existed, and so too have organized musical and other entertainments. Samuel Pepys used to go and see plays at the Red Bull in St John Street, Clerkenwell. In 1661 he was not too well pleased:

The play (which is called *All's Lost by Lust*) poorly done and with so much disorder, among others, that in the musique-room, the boy that was to sing a song not singing it right, his master fell about his eares and beat him so that put the whole house into an uprore.

Next year he was back with his wife to see *Dr Faustus* with little more success: "So wretchedly and poorly done, that we were sick of it." In fact, the only thing he ever seems to have enjoyed at the Red Bull was a prize fight.

That old tradition of bringing theatre to pubs is still alive. My good friends of The Mikron Theatre Company do just that, touring the waterways of England from April to September in

135

their fifty year old narrowboat and wintering in the Pennines from their home base in the Colne Valley. Not every performance is in a pub but in 1986 they played in 98 of them from, appropriately enough, the Narrow Boat at Islington to that old rival of the canals, the Railway at Marsden. Pub theatre is totally unlike the more conventional variety. Mikron have to take the pub as they find it: there will be those who have come along specially for the show, and others who are local regulars, who might well start off by resenting the intrusion. The company has to try and win them all over. Their shows are a mixture of serious themes and comedy, of speech and song. If at the end of the night the reluctant locals have been carried along and are joining in the last chorus with everyone else, then they know that they have won. Over the years they have built up their own loyal following, but just as importantly they have introduced live theatre to audiences who might otherwise never have experienced it at all. I think Samuel Pepys would have found Mikron theatre a great improvement over the players of Clerkenwell. Yet both are doing the same job: bringing theatre to the people instead of waiting for people to come to the theatre.

Mikron are, in fact, close to another tradition that grew up in close association with the pub, that of the music hall. In the nineteenth century it was common for various clubs and societies to meet in pubs and special club rooms were set aside for them. At other times the rooms could be let out for concert parties – and as the concert parties grew in popularity, so the space provided for them had to be extended. The movement apart of the hall for music and the bar was speeded up by the authorities who have always, it seems, taken a dim view of people actually enjoying themselves in pubs. So gradually the music rooms became theatres and the pubs stayed as pubs, though the old music hall stars were still great pubgoers in their spare time. And something of those days has always lingered on, for the pub remains the home of the not quite wholly respectable. The music is more likely to be jazz, born in the bars and brothels of New Orleans, than the string trio of the salon. Entertainment is often the red-nosed comic with the blue jokes or the stripper, and polite society looks the other way.

136

But without the toleration of the pub in the past for that on which officialdom frowned, there would have been no Marie Lloyd, no George Robey nor, on the other side of the Atlantic, would there have been a Mr Louis Armstrong. It will be a sad day for us all when the only entertainment a pub can offer is produced automatically at the turn of a switch or the press of a button.

An alehouse shown in a seventeenth-century pamphlet.

8. A Halfpennyworth of Bread and a deal of Sack

Item, A capon 2s 2d
Item, Sauce 4d
Item, Sack, two gallons 5s 8d
Item, Anchovies and sack after supper 2s 6d
Item, Bread .... ob.
O Monstrous! but one half-pennyworth of bread to this
intolerable deal of sack!

                                        Henry IV, Part I.

Falstaff's bar bill from the Boar's Head Tavern in Eastcheap is
probably the best known in the whole of English literature.
Whether, as Prince Hal clearly thinks, it is an appalling comment
on the old drunken knight that he maintained such a ratio
between solid and liquid intake or whether as others might
maintain he is keeping a right and proper relationship is one of
those subjects that can still be debated today. In other words, is
the pub to be a place that serves food with the occasional drink to
wash it down, or is it a place for drinkers who might occasionally
get hungry? Historically, the two have tended to exist side by
side, with first one then the other predominating. At the moment,
we seem to be in yet another period of transition with food taking
on an ever increasing importance. The old distinctions have
largely broken down – inn for food, accommodation and drink,
tavern for food and drink, alehouse for drink. Now everyone it
seems supplies food and just as the distinctions between the
different establishments have disappeared, so too the food
distinctions have vanished as well. The little pub that grew out of
the old alehouse might well serve food of far better quality than
the four star hotel that was once a roadside inn. Why should this
be so?

139

Go back in time and you will find the inn and tavern serving up food which differed little from that served up in a house of the same sort of status – grand food in grand inns, humble fare in humble inns. If you have to look for a period of rapid change, then you need turn back no further than Georgian times. Improved roads meant improved coach services and they in turn provided an encouragement for people to travel, not for businees, not on pilgrimage but for the pleasure of it. There was, in short, a tourist boom, and these tourists of the late eighteenth and early nineteenth century were wealthy people, prepared to spend some of that wealth on ensuring that eating whilst travelling was at least as pleasurable as eating at home.

There was a time when the inns of England were reckoned the best in the world. Would it were still so! Prince Pückler-Muskau, who visited the country several times from his home in Germany during the 1820s had nothing but praise for them.

In the country, even in small villages, you will find them equally neat and well attended. Cleanliness, great convenience and even elegance are always combined in them.

To prove his point he went on to describe what he was given for breakfast when all he had asked for was a pot of tea.

In the middle of the table smoked a large tea-urn, prettily surrounded by silver tea-canisters, a slop basin, and a milk-jug. There were three small Wedgwood plates, with as many knives and forks, and two cups of beautiful porcelain; by them stood an inviting plate of boiled eggs, another 'ditto' of broiled 'oreilles de cochon à la Sainte Menehould'; a plate of muffins, kept warm by a hot water-plate; another with cold ham; flaky white bread, dry and buttered toast, the best fresh butter in an elegant glass vessel; convenient receptacles for salt and pepper, English mustard and 'moutarde de maille'; lastly, a silver tea-caddy, with very good green and black tea.

That cost him 2 shillings, though I am not too sure about breaking
into French halfway through: one should not try and make an
oreille de cochon out of a sow's ear. Arriving in Britain at much
the same period a Dutch writer was regaled with much the same
meal and found everything at the inn to be of the same high
standard: "Oh", he said "if the rooms of the public inns are like
this, what must the apartments of the nobility be like!" He
decided to stay, wandered round the town in the morning and
came back with a hearty appetite:

Dinner was on the table when I came back, but soup and
table napkins I did not see. The waiter, the fat one, did stare
when I asked for these, but it appears that the White Hart did
not understand my wants, so I was forced to use my
handkerchief. But the table was crowded with things. It had
a cotton cloth quite clean, and many utensils which looked
like silver, including an epergne with glass dishes in which
were grapes, apples and sweetmeats. There was an immense
joint of roast beef at the head of the table, and a leg of mutton
of equal bulk at the bottom, both awaiting and defying the
guests. The table was set for ten persons, and each set of
knives and forks was flanked with two different sorts of fruit
pies. There were two large dishes of potatoes, and French
beans, and wedged among these was a mahogany waggon in
which rode an enormous Cheshire cheese. With the potatoes
was butter sauce, and in glass jars I did notice some pickled
onions and some walnuts, which gave a particular relish to
the beef. The company being seated, we fell to. For drink,
there was London porter, and for wine, some port, which I
found to be mixed with brandy. The meal over, three waiters
appeared and whipped the cloth from over our heads. It was
done so dexterously that no one seemed to mind. Then they
brought on the dessert – grapes, walnuts, apples – and
crackers, with a special service of highly decorative plates, as
well as napkins of checked pattern, evidently of wool, which
were of no use, and so with eating, drinking and talking, the
time did pass till tea was ready.

141

Tea indeed! How could he face another meal? But face it he did and retired to bed early, where one may assume he slept soundly until time came for a hearty breakfast. What a feast it sounds, but one cannot help wondering if all the inns were like this or whether he had been exceptionally lucky. There was no Egon Ronay to report in the 1820s, but a few travellers did jot down notes and among them was the great agriculturalist, Arthur Young who travelled through the north of England in the 1760s. Here is a selection of his comments:

> Rotherham. Crown. Very disagreeable and dirty. Hashed venison, potted mackerel, cold ham, cheese and melon, 1s.
> Leeds. King's Arms. Cook dirty. Veal cutlets, Tart and cheese. 8d. No beer.
> Driffield. Nag's Head. Civil and cheap. Mutton steaks, ducks, tarts, cheese, mushrooms, capers, walnuts, gherkins, and other pickles, 2s.
> Castle Howard. New Inn. Crowe. An excellent house, but dear and a saucy landlady.
> Newcastle. Extravagantly dear! Boiled fowl and oysters and one woodcock. 2s 6d.

A mixed bunch, but I do like the "extravagantly dear" comment at Newcastle. He should have tried a hotel I stayed at recently which cost over £50 a night for bed and breakfast, and all I got in the morning was a serve-yourself counter where the food had long dried up to a disgustingly leathery consistency. I was very glad someone else was paying the bill – and I didn't even get a saucy landlady.

It is easy to look back and romanticize the past, so here by way of correction is Robert Louis Stevenson at the Argyll Hotel in Iona with his friend Bough. They had been promised "nice broth, fresh herrings and fowl". It was Bough who was privileged to receive the first helping of the first course.

> How his face fell. 'I imagine myself in the accident ward of the Infirmary,' quoth he. It was, purely and simply, rice and

water. After this, we have another weary pause, and then herrings in a state of mash and potatoes like iron. 'Send the potatoes out to Prussia for grape-shot,' was the suggestion. I dined off broken herrings and dry bread. At last the supreme moment comes, and the fowl in a lovely dish is carried in. On the cover being raised, there is something so forlorn and miserable about the aspect of the animal that we both roar with laughter. Then Bough, taking up knife and fork, turns the "swarry" over and over, shaking doubtfully his head. 'There's an aspect of quiet resistance about the beggar," says he, "that looks bad." However, to work he falls, until the sweat stands on his brow, and a dismembered leg falls, dull and leaden-like, on to my dish. To eat was simply imposs-ible. I did not know before that flesh could be so tough. "The strongest jaws in England," says Bough piteously, harpoon-ing his dry morsel, "couldn't eat this leg in less than twelve hours." Nothing for it now, but to order boat and bill. "That fowl," says Bough to the landlady, "is of a breed I know. I knew the cut of its jib whenever it was put down. That was the grandmother of the cock that frightened Peter."

I recommend copying this passage, folding it neatly and placing it in your wallet or purse. Then, whenever anyone starts sounding off about pub food not being what it was in the old days, hand it over to them without further comment.

The inn and the tavern traditionally serve food in copious quantities, though as we have just seen not always of the very best quality. The alehouse provided for the working class in rather less grand style. In the nineteenth century a workman could turn up at his local on his way to work and hand over a piece of meat or a pie and then come back at midday to have it ready and waiting on a plate, knife and fork provided – no charge assuming of course that he swigged enough ale on the premises to make it worth the publican's while. It was inevitable that, in time, the landlord would begin to think that he had made a bad bargain, and the spread of the workman's caff helped change on its way. Charles

143

Booth in his London survey of 1888 described the process caught at the moment of change:

> The licensed victuallers begin to see that they cannot live by drink alone. Look more closely at the signs in their windows. There is hardly a window that does not show the necessity felt to cater for other wants besides drink. . . "Bovril" (a well advertised novelty) is to be had everywhere. Hot luncheons are offered, or a mid-day joint; or "sausage and mustard" are suggested to the hungry passer-by; at all events there will be sandwiches, biscuits, and bread and cheese.

The pub lunch had arrived. But it was all too soon to be followed by another familiar phenomenon described by our old friend Thomas Burke.

> Machine production of food and drink, like machine production of other things, gives us something slick and sterile; hygienic methods, admirable though they are, re-move not only imperfections but virtues . . . and in all departments of our daily needs, the touch of the human hand has been, or is being, obliterated – often on the plea that the human hand is insanitary. It may be; but I doubt that the human hand in its most soiled condition could produce less agreeable food than that produced by some hygienic machines.

Now we have all the elements gathered together that we might expect to find on the pub scene today. At one end of the scale is the inn, a role taken over by the modern hotel, an institution unlikely to bear a very close resemblance to its forebears. At the opposite extreme is the ordinary local, and in between every shade and variation is to be found. There are those pubs which have all but lost their pubby character, where the drinking fraternity are looked on as at best a necessary evil and all the emphasis now lies on the kitchen. There are former hotels which have come down in the world: where the bedrooms are now unused and where the groaning board has been replaced by a plastic dome beneath which long dead sandwiches curl up their toes towards the unpainted ceiling. Pub food shares many of the characteristics of British food in general – at its best it can be as good as any you will find in the world, at its worst . . . well, perhaps we should not dwell on that for too long. I have travelled all over Britain for many years, and at least there is one rule that I can lay down with absolute certainty. The quality of food you get in the pub has nothing whatsoever to do with the price you pay for it.

Before I sat down to write this chapter, I started to think of pubs where the food had been a truly memorable experience. I thought through those days of eating, and I realized that a pattern was starting to emerge. Now, I am not going to embark on a good food guide: this is all about experiences stretching over a long period. It only needs a change of ownership to turn yesterday's triumph into today's culinary disaster – or, if you are of an optimistic turn of mind, vice versa. So here we have some random jottings, and, let us begin, as one should at the beginning. I remember breakfasting after an overnight stay at Anstruther in Fife, where the landlord, who looked like a first cousin to James Robertson Justice, announced that he was just back from the harbour and would I like fresh fish? It proved, in fact, to be a far saner choice than the traditional fry-up as I spent much of the rest of the day bouncing around in heavy seas aboard a vintage fishing boat. Moving up towards what is certainly the main meal in the life of the pub, lunch, and one could go on for ever. I used to eat in a pub in London's Holborn, for example, which regularly featured tripe and onions on the menu. I recall a recent memorable encounter with a steak and kidney pudding, served with fresh, crisp vegetables in Faversham in Kent. Often, too, the simplest food can seem the best. Out walking in the Derbyshire hills, I found plain bread and cheese, but the bread was home-made, the cheese came from a farm up the road, the butter came in a little earthenware pot and not in foil you can never get unwrapped, and the pickled onions had never seen the inside of a factory. I imagine by now that the gist of the argument is

145

becoming clear. These were traditional meals using local, fresh produce and, just as importantly in context, they went superbly with beer.

I enjoy good food, and if I am going out to a restaurant for an evening I am as likely to go to an Indonesian as an Italian, but I would not wish, as a rule, to eat food from either country in a pub. It seems odd to me that those who snigger in a rather superior way at people who order steak and chips in an Indian restaurant, think it quite reasonable to order chicken vindaloo in an English pub. Personally, I feel much the same in both places: people are free to eat whatever they like. What is happening today, however, is that there is often less chance for me to find what I like. Out have gone the old dishes and in have come the ubiquitous lasagnes and chilli con carne – I once had to work with someone who had lunched on chilli and draught Bass. It is not an experience I should care to repeat. The change has happened and it will be difficult to turn back the clock, but there is surely a place somewhere for food that fits with the surroundings and goes with what is still the main beverage of the pub – beer.

If you want to know what is happening now and what is likely to happen in the future, you could either visit a hundred pubs, which is a tempting prospect but perhaps a little impractical, or go to one caterer who supplies a hundred pubs. I chose the latter course and trotted along to a converted cowshed in Noke near Oxford to find the charmingly alliterative Country Cottage Catering.

Peter Marsh and Joy Barker set up in business in 1983 because they reckoned they had identified a real need. Almost anyone in the pub trade will tell you that these days it is increasingly difficult to make a living if you don't do food. The small pub rarely has the facilities for catering on a large scale – hence the appeal of the old ploughman's lunch and the sandwich. The microwave oven seemed the best thing since sliced bread. Unhappily, what comes out of many microwaves is also just about as appetizing as sliced bread: the computer adage "rubbish in – rubbish out" – proved equally true of the new catering. Country Cottage wanted to provide food of good quality at a reasonable price which could be microwaved or reheated in a conventional oven without any loss of flavour. It also had to look good and suggest that somewhere behind the bar was an apple-cheeked, stout lady in a pinafore who had been working away with local produce. If you have ever wondered why the "home-cooked" food in pub A seems identical to that in pub B a few miles away, it might well be because neither specifies exactly whose home it was cooked in. Country Cottage is just one of a number of concerns which could be the answer.

The best thing about Country Cottage is that they really do provide good food. I sat down with Peter Marsh in his kitchen to try the chicken liver pate and a glass of wine, and I must say the pate was superb. We have made chicken liver pate at home and there is no mistaking the real thing when you get it. But I don't go to pubs for pate and wine. On the other hand, I liked the sound of Half Pay Pie described in their trade list as a "hearty old English dish consisting of beef, beer and barley simmered gently together and topped with a half circle of puff pastry". I would be equally happy with their beef and Guinness pie or any of their other "individual pies". It is a pleasure to find the name "individual pie" applied to a concoction made with first-rate ingredients in much the same way as it might be at home, in a pie dish. Indeed, the only difference is that here they cook in large batches rather than one at a time. After cooking they are fast frozen and then reheated at the pub. When you think of what used to pass as pies and sometimes still goes, a hideous mass-produced object of soggy pastry, glutinous gravy and the gristly remains of the one that came last in the 2.30 at Newmarket – the new version has to be good news.

In an ideal world, each pub would have fresh food, freshly prepared. It can still be found and where it is found it is to be loved and cherished. The world, alas, is not ideal and I for one would be quite happy to lunch out on Half Pay Pie. Would I even know that I was eating caterer's food, frozen and reheated? I have to admit that I recently had an excellent Ploughman's Pie made up of eight different vegetables and I even complimented the landlord on the cooking of it. He smiled politely and accepted the praise. Yes, it was Country Cottage. So this seems to me to be an excellent compromise and I am even prepared, generous soul that

I am, to accept chicken in cheese, tarragon and white wine – though I cannot believe it goes well with a pint of best bitter – so long as they go on doing a good steak and kidney. But there are other more powerful forces at work in the land, who have a very different viewpoint. Peter Marsh and Joy Barker believe that they thrive because they combine the provision of good food with a very businesslike attitude to going out and selling it to the pub. Others have different priorities.

Talk to others in the brewing and catering business and the phrases that you hear time and time again tend to be about portion control and profit margins – with very little about what finishes up on the punter's plate. Pub food looks like being yet another victim of the big, monopolistic breweries. It is all part of the same trend that looks for managers not tenants and then imposes strict controls on how a place is run. Food policy then becomes the concern of accountants who don't know their aspics from their endives – and that policy does not have a place either for home cooking on the premises, or the small caterer. For these culinary hatchet men, the ideal caterer is the one who offers the best trade terms, for the flow of cash is of infinitely greater importance than the flow of gastric juices. The small people simply cannot afford to wait for payment so they lose out – and more importantly, we, the customers, lose out. There is a vision of the future where everyone gets a standard meal of a standard size at a standard price. What other prospects are on offer?

I have just been looking through the Country Cottage list and I was struck by the mixture being offered. The lasagnes and moussakas, the beef Provençal and the Cantonese chicken. There seems to be a message about where the pub lunch is heading and Peter Marsh has no doubt about it. He is certain that the emphasis is going to shift from the pub as a place that sells drinks and provides some food towards a place that sells food and the drinks to go with it. Ultimately, he sees the pub as becoming something much closer to the continental cafe. I hope he is wrong, but I have a horrible suspicion that he is right – and if he is then something unique and valuable will have been lost. Quite recently I stopped at a pub and was told to take a seat and the menu would be brought to me. If this sort of thing spreads then the pub is doomed, for if we are all to be sat at tables and told to stay put then there is an end to conversation among strangers, an end to the pub game – waiters don't want darts in the soup – an end to the days when the landlord set the atmosphere of the pub. Perhaps I am taking an unusually gloomy view of the situation because I live in southern England, for the trend towards "restaurantization" is much stronger here than in the rest of Britain. Perhaps the time has come for a Campaign for Real Pub Food, which would suffer from the disadvantage that you cannot pronounce CAMRPF without producing the sort of noise that you get after chilli con carne and Bass.

But it would be a pity to end on a note of gloom, for the tradition of serving good, plain, wholesome food has been with us for a very long time and may yet survive the snares set by accountants. The following is from a phrase book of useful conversations for French visitors visiting an English inn:

Mine host, when shall we sup? I have a good stomach.
When it shall please you, sir. It is fasting day to-day – it is our Lady's even. There are eggs in the shell, buttered, poached, and fried.
I must eat some flesh, for I love not eggs or fish.
Then there is a very good caponet. There is a fat capon, a Turkey-cock, a fat goose, a dozen of larks, a couple of good fat rabbits. There is a good lamprey, and here is the side of a salmon.
To you, mine host. To you, mine hostess. I will pledge you here.

We should certainly lift our glasses in a toast to any host of today who could offer as much.

John Gilpin galloping past the Bell at Edmonton.

9. Mermaids and other Literary Beasts

Souls of poets dead and gone,
What Elysium have ye known,
Happy field or mossy cavern
Choicer than the Mermaid Tavern?

John Keats

Keats looked back to the great days of Elizabethan England when a group of men met at a London tavern to exchange stories, match witticisms and discuss the life of a theatre of which they were the luminaries. Shakespeare and Ben Jonson, Christopher Marlowe and Francis Beaumont were all there at various times, and the life of the tavern was to find a place in their works. If Keats saw it as some impossibly wonderful gathering of brilliant men, then he was doing no more than repeat the views of the contemporaries who knew its golden hour. These lines were written by Beaumont to Jonson.

What things have we seen,
Done at the Mermaid! Heard words that have been
So nimble, and so full of subtle flame,
As if that every one from whence they came
Had meant to put his whole wit in a jest,
And had resolved to live a fool the rest
Of his dull life.

The merrymakers of the Mermaid found inspiration in the tavern, and repaid the compliment by praising the tavern in words. They were not alone in this and writers through the years have done the same. This chapter presents a few highlights from the printed page, and introduces a few pubs and inns that have associations with the famous.

We have already met the most famous of all medieval poets, Geoffrey Chaucer, and his company gathered at the Tabard for the pilgrimage to Canterbury: and a very jolly place it seems to be. His great contemporary Langland in *Piers Plowman* paints a quite different picture. He described the London street scene where the cries rang out to tempt the passers-by:

Cooks to their knaves cried "Hot pies, hot!
Good grisken [pork] and geese – go dine, go!"
Taverners unto them told the same tale –
White wine of Oseye, and red wine of Gascoyne,
Of the Rhine and of Rochelle, the roast meat to digest.

It still sounds very entertaining, but once Langland takes us into the tavern full of drunks and whores and, to his extreme displeasure, clergy, things take on a quite different hue. He ends by branding the brewer as one of those who "most harm worketh to the poor". In fact, it seems as much as anything to have been the sight of the drunken priests that angered Langland. John Wycliff was even sterner on this point. I have somewhat modernized his tirade to make it intelligible, but the anger still shows through.

The clergy . . . haunt taverns out of all measure and stir lewd men to drunkenness, idleness and cursed swearing and drinking and fighting. They fall to stupid games at table, chess and hazard, and beat the streets, and sit at the tavern till they have lost their wit, and then chide and stride and fight, and sometime neither eye nor tongue nor hand nor foot to help themselves for drunkenness.

I rather like the last part of this tirade, a sort of elongated medieval way of saying that the vicar was legless.

The tavern always seems to have partaken of this dual character: on the one hand Chaucer's convivial company, on the other Langland's idling drunks. They meet and combine in Shakespeare, who does not take sides but simply presents the picture in the round, the good and bad, the lowlife wastrels and

152

the aristrocratic merrymakers. Falstaff's favourite haunt the Boar's Head seems real – and it was real. Shakespeare gives us the cries of the tavern – "Anon, anon, sir! Score a pint of bastard in the Half-moon", and the language of the drawers who "call drinking deep, dyeing scarlet" and adds a dozen more phrases to show his complete familiarity with this world. How the English Tourist Board must wish the old tavern was still standing, but it went, knocked down in 1831 to make way for a new approach to London Bridge. The house where Falstaff drank sack and canary with Prince Hal and Mistress Quickly was replaced by a statue of William IV – a poor exchange.

Somehow, religion and the alehouse seemed to get mixed up together again after the Restoration, and man-about-town Ned Ward of *The London Spy* described a visit to a London tavern which he and his friend found occupied by Puritans. The two groups viewed each other with mutual distaste.

> They leering at us under their Bongraces, with as much contempt, as so many *Primitive Christians* at a couple of *Pagans*.
>
> We, like true Protestant Topers, who scorn the Hippocrisie of tipling by half pints, as if we Drank rather to wash away our *Sins* than our *Sorows*, appear'd bare-fac'd, call'd for a Quart at once, and soon discover'd our Religion by our Drinking; whilst they, like true Puritans, gifted with abundance of holy cheats, will never be Catch'd over more than half a Pint, tho's they'll drink Twenty at a Sitting. . .
>
> Thus did the licorice Saints quaff it round as merrily, after their precise and Canting manner as so many Country Parsons over a Tub of Ale, when freed from the remarks of their censorious Parishoners, till, like reprobate Sinners, who have not the fear of Providence before their Eyes, they were deluded by Satan into a wicked state of Drunkenness.

The clergy of the eighteenth century were not always averse to a tipple, and the most famous of them all Jonathan Swift found time to jot down verses in pubs and about pubs. He visited The Rose at

Wokingham with a selection of literary friends – John Arbuthnot, John Gray and Alexander Pope. The landlord's daughter rather took their fancy and they set out to write verses in her honour which they left behind as a sort of literary tip for their pretty barmaid. They produced classical verses.

> Were Virgil alive with his Phyllis
> And writing another Eclogue
> Both his Phyllis and fair Amaryllis
> He'd give up for sweet Molly Mog

And verses that were somewhat more down to earth.

> The schoolboy's desire is a play day:
> The schoolmaster's joy is to flog;
> The milkmaid's delight is a May Day
> But mine is on sweet Molly Mog.

The pub is still there, though not much of its age shows in its face. Swift is also said to have obliged his barber with a verse, when that gentleman in the best Irish tradition decided that selling beer would add greatly to his income from shaves and haircuts, and would be more amusing for his customers than last year's periodicals. The lines do not sound very Swiftian, but they pleased The Jolly Barber and adorned his sign.

> Rove not from pole to pole, but step in here,
> Where naught excells the shaving but the beer.

Already too, by this time, there were writers ready to extol the virtues of good British ale whatever the poor benighted foreigners might think. Congreve even wrote a song on the subject in *Love for Love*

> Prithee fill me the glass
> Till it laugh in my face,
> He that whines for a lass

Is an ignorant ass,
For a bumper has not a fellow
. . . .
To drink is a Christian diversion
Unknown to the Turk or the Persian:
Let Mahometan fools
Live by heathenish rules,
And be damned over tea-cups and coffee;
Let the British lads sing,
Crown a health to the king,
And a fig for your Sultan and Sophy.

There were, however, other aspects of the age which were to appeal to the writers of the next century as suitable subjects for romance and adventure: the world of pirates, smugglers and highwaymen. No-one has ever written a better pirate story than Robert Louis Stevenson's *Treasure Island* and it is doubtful if anyone ever will – and inns play an important part in the tale. Long John Silver is landlord of the Spyglass when we first meet him, a tavern full of sailors and the tang of the sea. But it is at the lonely inn on the coast, the Admiral Benbow, that the story first gets into its stride with the arrival of the sea captain.

I remember him as if it were yesterday, as he came plodding to the inn door, his sea-chest following behind him in a hand-barrow; a tall, strong, heavy, nut-brown man; his tarry pigtail falling over the shoulders of his soiled blue coat; his hands ragged and scarred, with black, broken nails; and the sabre cut across one cheek, a dirty, livid white. I remember him looking round the cove and whistling to himself as he did so, and then breaking out in that old sea-song that he sang so often afterwards:
"Fifteen men on the dead man's chest" –
Yo-ho-ho, and a bottle of rum!
in the high, old tottering voice that seemed to have been tuned and broken at the capstan bars. Then he rapped on the door with a bit of stick like a handspike that he carried, and

155

when my father appeared, called roughly for a glass of rum. This, when it was brought to him, he drank slowly, like a connoisseur, lingering on the taste, and still looking about him at the cliffs and up at our signboard.

"This is a handy cove", says he, at length; "and a pleasant sittyated grog-shop. Much company, mate?"

My father told him no, very little company, the more was the pity.

"Well, then," said he, "this is the berth for me".

Pirates were only occasional visitors to inns – smugglers made them their headquarters, and if the number of reputed old smugglers' inns around the coast are any indication, then it must have been a well populated profession. Russell Thorndike based his *Dr. Syn* novels on Rye in Sussex, where every old pub and inn claims to be a smugglers retreat and probably was. The most prominent was The Mermaid, headquarters of the Hawkhurst Gang, and when you read of their doings you find historical truth outstripping even Thorndike's imaginative descriptions. It is the sheer scale of the operations that astonishes. A former smuggler gave evidence that in the eighteenth century there were some twenty thousand in the trade and that no-one could do anything against such numbers,

> in particular at the village of Hawkhurst, Kent, 500 can get together armed, in less than an hour: that not one person in ten in the country but would give them assistance, and do lend the smugglers their horses and teams to convey their goods.

Thorndike's fictitious smugglers go to elaborate lengths to hide their identities; the real smugglers of The Mermaid went about their business more or less openly. When a troop of soldiers was sent to help the hard-pressed customs officers, it was not the army who attacked the smugglers, but the smugglers who attacked the army. They overpowered them, took away all their weapons and marched in triumph through the streets with banners flying. Not much secrecy there! So, next time you go to an old smugglers inn, don't think so much of secret passages but rather of an open trade carried on with the support of respected customers. Nowadays, of course, the worst that the customs officer is likely to find in a pub in Rye is a mistake in the VAT returns – and no-one has yet found anything romantic about that.

The eighteenth century also saw the arrival of the inn in a role which it was to perform and go on performing right up to the present day: as a setting for farce. The confusions that can be caused by many people staying in many rooms, and not always being found quite where they should be, have been played out on the stage, notably in the works of Ben Travers, and in the novel. The honour of being first in line would seem to belong to a genuine inn, The White Lion at Upton-on-Severn. It features in Fielding's *Tom Jones* where the hero brings Mrs Waters whom he has recently rescued from a fate worse than death – and who she rewards by cheerfully submitting to that same fate, at which point the husband arrives on the scene. Only she is not, it soon appears, the errant wife after all. The landlady, anxious to preserve the reputation of her inn, convinces everyone that Tom and Mrs Waters are respectable folk, with this irrefutable argument:

> I would not have believed my own eyes against such good gentlefolks. I have not had a better supper ordered this half year than they ordered last night, and so easy and good-humoured were they, that they found no fault with my Worcestershire perry, which I sold them for champagne; and to be sure it is as well tasted, and as wholesome as the best champagne in the kingdom, otherwise I would scorn to give it 'em, and they drank me two bottles. No, no, I will never believe any harm of such sober good sort of people.

There were two faces to the eighteenth century: the rumbustious, high living bawdy of *Tom Jones* is one, the harshness of the life of the poor is the other. Both found expression in Oliver Gold-smith's works. *The Deserted Village* tells of the death of a community killed off by greedy landlords, and among the victims was the old inn.

> Low lies that house where nut-brown draughts inspired,
> Where grey-beard mirth and smiling toil retired;
> Where village statesmen talked with looks profound;
> And news, much older than the Ale, went round.
> Obscure it sinks, nor shall it more impart
> An hour's importance to a poor man's heart.

But Goldsmith did his drinking in the Globe in Fleet Street and this it is said was his favourite song.

> Fair Venus the goddess of beauty and love
> Arose from the froth that swam on the sea,
> Minerva leap'd out of the cranium of Jove,
> A coy sullen slut, as most authors agree;
> Bold Bacchus they tell us, the prince of good fellows,
> Was his natural son, but attend to my tale,
> For they that thus chatter mistake quite the matter,
> He sprang from a barrel of Nottingham ale.
>   Nottingham ale, boys; Nottingham ale;
>   No liquor on earth is like Nottingham ale.

North of the border it was not the delights of Nottingham, nor any other ale that were hymned. Scotland's greatest poet dipped his pen in the ink more than once to praise the worth of Scotland's greatest drink. Burns showed himself to share the Kentish man's contempt for the liquor laws of the day:

> There's threesome reels, there's foursome reels,
> There's hornpipes and strathspeys, man,
> But the ae best dance e'er cam to the Land
> Was, the de'il's awa wi th' Exciseman.

Or to put more succinctly

> Freedom and Whisky gang thegither.

Whisky runs through his work like a stream through the heather: it gave Tam o'Shanter courage for his adventures and it oiled the machinery of friendship.

> Oh! Willie brew'd a peck o'maut,
> An Rob a' Allan cam' to pree;
> Three blyther hearts, that lee long night,
> Ye wad na find in Christendie.
> We are na fou, we're nae that fou,
> But just a drappie in our e'e;
> The cock may craw, the day may daw,
> And aye we'll taste the Whasky O.

Burns can no more be read without a dram than haggis can be eaten or Auld Lang Syne sung without a similar accompaniment. No writer has ever been more eloquent on his native drink than Robert Burns on the malt. Naturally enough, he had his own favourite watering holes including Poosie Nansie's in Mauchline and the Globe Inn in Dundee.

The poets of the nineteenth century are, in popular imagination, thought of as having their minds on higher things than the boozer round the corner or the pub at the end of the country lane. Yet even the exalted Wordsworth could, it seems, be persuaded to turn a few lines to celebrate a new sign at his local, especially when it was the work of the landlord's own hand. If the quality of the verse is anything to go by, he took his payment in liquid form – and took his glass in hand before his pen.

> Who does not know the famous Swan,
> Object uncouth and yet our boast,
> For it was painted by the host?
> His own conceit, the figure planned,
> 'Twas coloured all by his own hand.

After verse like that it is a pleasure to turn back to prose. Novelists soon realized that the great attraction of the pub or inn as a place where all kinds of varieties of people could meet by accident in a free and easy atmosphere also makes it a most useful rendezvous for fictional characters. You can scarcely open a nineteenth-century novel without finding inns and taverns creeping into the narrative. George Eliot knew them well and at the beginning of *Felix Holt The Radical* she sounds a note that had been sounded for as long as inns have been discussed – things are not what they were.

> Five-and-thirty years ago the glory had not yet departed from the old coach-road: the great roadside inns were still brilliant with well-polished tankards, the smiling glances of pretty barmaids, and the repartees of jocose ostlers; the mail still announced itself by the merry notes of the horn; the hedge-cutter or the rick-thatcher might still know the exact hour by the unfailing yet otherwise meteoric apparition of the pea-green Tally-ho or the yellow Independent; and elderly gentlemen in pony-chaises, quartering nervously to make way for the rolling swinging swiftness, had not ceased to remark that times were finely changed since they used to see the pack-horses and hear the tinkling of their bells on this very highway.

She also knew all about "the strong ale" enjoyed by the miners in The Sugar Loaf and "the muddier drink" that wet the navvies' thirst in The Blue Cow.

No-one, however, has done more to set the image of the coaching inn and the town pub of Victorian England than Charles Dickens. The potential of the inn as a home for farce that first appeared in *Tom Jones* achieved fulfilment in *The Pickwick Papers*. Take the chance meetings in inns out of that book and the whole narrative would collapse round your ears. There is no need to quote his descriptions, we have already had a fair sample, but what strikes one is the vivid nature of his portraits. They seem to be drawn from life – and so they were. Whole books have been written about Dickens' inns – indeed, a gentleman by the name of B. W. Matz managed a whole book on Pickwick alone. But take just one example from another work, the Saracen's Head in Snow

Hill, London where Nicholas Nickleby first met Mr Wackford Squiers and you find that it was indeed based on a genuine Saracen's Head, and one with an interesting history of its own. It was said to have been given its name at the end of the twelfth century when Richard I stopped there on his way to the Crusades. He drank a few jars until, as the chronicler put it, "ye hedde of ye Kinge did swimme righte royallie", at which point the royal tippler began putting in some sword practice on the furniture. "I wish", said one of the accompanying barons, "hys Majestie hadde ye hedde of a Saracen before hym juste now, for I trowe he woulde play ye deuce wyth itte." Next day the king paid for the damages and renamed the inn.

If Dickens can take the prize as laureate of the inn then the award for extolling the virtues of the honest pub and good ale must go to George Borrow. In *Wild Wales* he describes walking from one end of the country to the other, and from choice he would always settle for the plain comforts of the plain pub and the conversation of the country people he met there. Taking just one stop from a long tour, here he is at the end of a long day's walking at the pub in Pumpsaint, between Lampeter and Llandovery.

> I entered the inn of the "Pump-Saint". It was a comfortable old-fashioned place, with a very large kitchen and a rather small parlour. The people were kind and attentive, and soon set before me in the parlour a homely but savoury supper and a foaming tankard of ale. After supper I went into the kitchen, and sitting down with the good folks in an immense chimney-corner, listened to them talking in their Carmarthenshire dialect till it was time to go to rest, when I was conducted to a large chamber where I found an excellent and clean bed awaiting me in which I enjoyed a refreshing sleep.

There is still a homely pub at Pumpsaint, though you no longer get invited into the kitchen. Recently I went walking on the route taken by Borrow and I was pleased to find many of the pubs and inns he called in at were still there and still offering the same simple pleasures. Not that Borrow found everything to his liking wherever he went. In Chester, he vowed to try Cheshire cheese which he found to have "much the appearance of soap" and a similar flavour. That went straight out of the window. He then turned to the ale which soon followed the cheese, after which he went on to quote an old rhyme about the local beer:

Chester ale, Chester ale! I could ne'er get it down,
'Tis made of ground-ivy, of dirt, and of bran,
'Tis as thick as a river below a huge town!
'Tis not lap for a dog, far less drink for a man.

There are times when you are following in another's tracks and you are heartily relieved to find that some things at least have changed for the better. Much of Chester may have been taken over by Greenall Whitley, which can be quite a decent drop, especially when provided by the Wem Brewery, but you can find the occasional alternative. The Olde Custom House is one of those half-timbered buildings for which the city is famous, and there they purvey Marston's. Mr Borrow would not, I think, have shot his pint of Pedigree out of the window.

Creeping over into the twentieth century, one at first sniffs only the rather faint aroma of nostalgia, and an even stronger whiff of gentility. Rupert Brooke, who is better remembered for his enquiries as to whether there was honey still for tea at ten past three in Grantchester, seems to have found something to his liking in the Fleur de Lys at Cranborne in Dorset. It does not, however, seem to have been the beer that stirred his memory.

We somewhere missed the faces bright,
The lips and eyes we longed to see;
And Love and Laughter and Delight.
These things are at the Fleur de Lys.

I like to think of that as a hymn to the barmaids, but it probably wasn't. Arnold Bennett writing of the Five Towns took a much more down to earth view of pubs and the ladies who served there.

In one of his short stories he describes a visit to the private bar of the Tiger at Bursley.

It was a small and low room. I instinctively stooped, though there was no necessity for me to stoop. The bar had no peculiarity. It can be described in a breath: Three perpendicular planes. Back plane, bottles arranged exactly like books on bookshelves; middle plane, the upper halves of two women dressed in tight black; front plane, a counter, dotted with glasses and having strange areas of zinc. . . A private bar is as eternal as the hills, as changeless as the monomania of a madman, as mysterious as sorcery. Always the same order of bottles, the same tinkling, the same popping, the same timetable, and the same realistic pictures of frothing champagne on the walls, the same advertisements on the same ash-trays on the counter, the same odour that wipes your face like a towel the instant you enter; and the same smiles, the same gestures, the same black fabric stretched to tension over the same impressive mammiferous phenomena of the same inexplicable creatures who apparently never eat and never sleep, imprisoned for life in the hallowed and mystic hollow between the bottles and the zinc.

The Tiger at Bursley is the thinly disguised Leopard of Burslem. It still exists, and you might care to check out the description though I would not recommend too close an inspection of any impressive mammiferous phenomena you might happen to encounter.

The twentieth century also produced two writers who were to become champions of the British Way of Drinking. One we have already met, G. K. Chesterton; the second is Hilaire Belloc. He lived down at Shipley in Sussex – where he was proud possessor of a windmill – and he obviously sampled widely.

They sell good beer at Haslemere
And under Guildford Hill
At Little Cowfold I've been told

A beggar may drink his fill:
There is a good brew in Amberley too,
And by the bridge also;
But the swipes they take in at Washington Inn
Is the very best Beer I know.

Things have changed a little in Sussex, just like everywhere else and of the fifty odd brewers you could once find, only King and Barnes now survive, though a few recent newcomers have appeared to add a touch of variety to the scene. And there are still some good pubs to be found. And that at least would have pleased Mr Belloc who was the author of the famous and very true lines:

When you have lost your inns, drown your empty selves for you will have lost the last of England.

This is one of those grand statements designed to get us all up on our feet and cheering – but what do we actually think of as the inns of England? I know what I think when I read those words. I think of an old building reached only with difficulty at the end of some half forgotten sunken lane. I think of floors supported by beams that were carved out of the ancient forests – of fires in a hearth where fires burnt bright when the beacons were lit to warn of the approaching Armada; of beer drawn from the wood and honest fare at honest prices. It is probably a mirage. The transition between the old and ye olde is caught in fiction in Eric Linklater's *Poet's Pub*. It begins promisingly enough with a description of how the pub got its name; a story which can be repeated with variations at a hundred different pubs.

They call it "The Downy Pelican" now, but that isn't its original name. It started as "The Tabard". Then the three dullest poets of the seventeenth century happened to live in Downish – Fabian Metcalf, Philip Goode, and Martin Stout – and they drank in the Tabard and recited their ridiculous mock-metaphysical verses to each other and to the landlord, who had literary aspirations. He thought well of them, for they spent their money there and they wrote verses of a kind which he couldn't, though he wanted to, and in their honour he re-christened his inn "The Downish Helicon," which so far as I know was his one literary excursion. But Philip Goode died, and Martin Stout and Metcalf and the landlord died, and no-one remembered them, and the inn sign grew battered, and the villagers thought nothing of so strange a name and could never learn to pronounce it. So when the eighteenth century was nearly finished a new landlord had the sign re-painted and lettered with what he took to be its proper name, "The Downy Pelican". And that's what it's called today.

It all sounds very splendid and traditional, but as we learn more and more about the Downy Pelican we soon discover that it is suffering from a creeping, insidious infection which I call "modernevialism". It is an odd complaint, which arises when innkeepers are tempted to unite two apparent irreconcilables – a love of the past and a desire to pander to every whim of the moment. So we find the poetic landlord presiding over an American bar in the buttery where cocktails are the order of the day, whilst planning medieval banquets full of items like "kickshawses" and "marrowbone pie", designed to appeal to an international clientele looking for the genuine "olde worlde" experience. We have not solved the problem yet, of how to retain the best of the old whilst keeping open minds about the best of the new. I do not think, however, I should have enjoyed it any more than I should enjoy its latter day equivalent, the medieval banquet at which the drinking of a nauseous concoction of mead is inescapable. But we should be grateful to Eric Linklater for recording that moment when modernism and medievalism met head on in the English inn.

The early twentieth century was also the age which saw the finest flowering of a new literary genre – the detective story. There were numerous variations around at the time, including the American version exemplified by Raymond Chandler and Dashiell Hammett, which had a basis in reality and was set in the seamier areas where real crimes occur. The English country house mystery was a quite different matter, an elaborate crossword puzzle of a story where the hero was never the professional policeman but always the amateur lady or gentleman. Class distinction, however, created real problems for the writers. The plot might involve the murder of Lord Blank and the chief suspect might be the Hon. Reginald Cipher-Cipher, but one could not ignore the fact that the witnesses might include the waiter, the porter and the upstairs maid. Where could you go to catch the underlings off guard and who could do the questioning? In Dorothy Sayers' classic Lord Peter Wimsey stories, it is the role of the butler Bunter to make contacts at the local.

At the entrance of the stranger, the voices, which had been busy, fell silent, and glances, at first directed to the door, were swiftly averted and screened behind lifted tankards. This was fully in accordance with etiquette. Bunter saluted the company with a polite "Good evening," and asked for a pint of old ale and a packet of Players. Mr Gudgeon, the landlord, fulfilled the order with a dignified leisure, observing, as he changed a ten-shilling note, that the day had been fine. Bunter assented to this proposition, saying further that the country air was agreeable after town. Mr Gudgeon remarked that a-many London gentlemen had been known to say the same thing, and inquired whether this was his customer's first visit to that part of the country. Bunter said that though he had frequently passed through the district he had never stayed there before, and that Paggleham seemed to be a pretty spot. He also volunteered the information that he was Kentish by birth. Mr Gudgeon said, Indeed? they grew hops there, he believed. Bunter admitted that this was so. A very stout man with one eye intervened at this point to say that his wife's cousin lived in Kent, and that it was all 'ops where he was. Bunter said there were hops where his mother lived.

The niceties of pub etiquette having been observed, Bunter is now free to probe into the mystery and establish the local views. The pub continues to crop up in such stories, simply because it is the one point of contact between the social classes – between the ingenious murderer and his aristocratic victims on the one hand and the spectating lower orders, who cannot see the significance of their observations until the Amateur Gentleman had made all plain. The Sayers view of the pub smacks of the writer looking down on a lower form of life; a view not untypical in the writing of the interwar years. Inevitably, the better the writer, the more accurate a picture you are likely to get – even if it is not always very flattering. Who can say that they have not seen a bar such as Leopold Bloom saw, nor felt the nausea he felt, as described in James Joyce's vivid portrayal of a day in Dublin in *Ulysses*.

Perched on high stools by the bar, hats shoved back, at the tables calling for more bread no charge, swilling, wolfing gobfuls of sloppy food, their eyes bulging, wiping wetted moustaches. A pallid suetfaced young man polished his tumbler knife fork and spoon with his napkin. New set of microbes. A man with an infant's saucestained napkin tucked round him shovelled gurgling soup down his gullet. A man spitting back on his plate: halfmasticated gristle: no teeth to chewchewchew it. Chump chop from the grill. Bolting to get it over. Sad booser's eyes. Bitten off more than he can chew. Am I like that?

Well, am I? Are you? We have all been there and we can all recognize the "Smells of men . . . sweetish warmish cigarette smoke, reek of plug, spilt beer, men's beery piss, the stale of ferment."

The romantic aura that surrounded the pub seemed to die away in the latter half of the century. It remained a meeting place for writers such as the Oxford Group that gathered at the Eagle and Child, popularly known as the Bird and Baby. The Inklings, as the group was called, included J. R. R. Tolkien, but not much of real pub life permeated through into the tales of hobbits and

Middle Earth, though inns and taverns do pop up from time to time. The literary divorce between an idealized old world pub and reality seemed to be absolute. Even Dylan Thomas, who had fallen out of more pubs than most poets had ever entered, created an idealized ever open pub in the village of Llaregyb or Milk Wood.

Up the street, in the Sailors Arms, Sinbad Sailors, grandson of Mary Ann Sailors, draws a pint in the sunlit bar. The ship's clock in the bar says half past eleven, half past eleven is opening time. The hands of the clock have stayed still at half-past eleven for fifty years. It is always opening time in the Sailors Arms.

It was Kingsley Amis in *Lucky Jim* who seems to have brought the ordinary pub we can all recognize back into literature – a place where Jim can go to escape the mock medievalism of his appalling professor – just as a real life drinker of today might wish to escape the mock medievalism of Eric Linklater's Poets' Pub, with its glasses of lamb's wool and malmsey.

Writers through the ages have described pubs, celebrated or decried pubs and, on the whole, set up a mirror that has accurately reflected society's attitudes towards pubs. And it is the writer who has the very last words of all – the writer of epitaphs. I cannot think of a better one than this written in Latin in the twelfth century and translated by Helen Waddell.

For on this my heart is set;
When the hour is nigh me
Let me in the tavern die,
With a tankard by me,
While the angels looking down
Joyously sing o'er me,
Deus sit propitius
Huic potatori.

Acknowledgements

The author and publishers wish to thank the following for the use of their illustrations in the book: the BBC Hulton Picture Library for the picture on page 42; the Bodleian Library, Oxford, for the use of illustrations on the title page and pages 16, 64, 122, 138 and 150; Collins, publishers of *The English Pub* by Michael Jackson for the endpiece; Mary Evans Picture Library for illustrations on pages 86 and 106; and The Guildhall Library for that on page 6.

They would also like to thank the following for kindly giving permission for the use of copyright material: The Bodley Head and the Estate of James Joyce for the extract from *Ulysses;* Jonathan Cape Ltd for the extract from *Poet's Pub* by Eric Linklater; J. M. Dent for the extract from *Under Milk Wood* by Dylan Thomas; Duckworth & Co. Ltd for the extract from *This That and The Other* by Hilaire Belloc; Faber & Faber Ltd for the extract from *Collected Poems 1909–1962* by T. S. Eliot and for the extract from *An Innkeeper's Diary* by John Fothergill; Victor Gollancz Ltd for the extract from *The Pub and The People* by Mass Observation, reprinted by kind permission of the Mass Observation Archive, and for the extract from *Busman's Honeymoon* by Dorothy Sayers; Macmillan for the extract from *England, Their England* by A. G. Macdonell; John Murray (Publishers) Ltd for the extract from "The Dear Old Village" in Collected Poems by John Betjeman; Routledge & Kegan Paul for the extract from *Will Someone Lead Me to a Pub*.

Thanks to Pip Burton for the picture research.

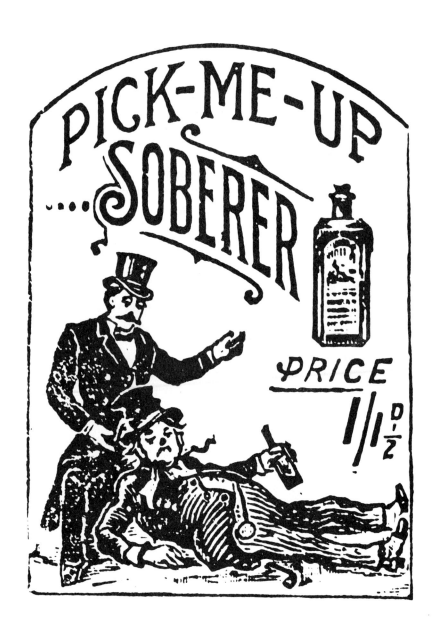

Index